Jerry Pearlman[*]

The Death of the Common Attorney

---

[*] A.k.a. J. J. Pearlman M.B.E. Ll,B, Solicitor of the Supreme Court

novum pro

www.novum-publishing.co.uk

All rights of distribution, including via film, radio, and television, photomechanical reproduction, audio storage media, electronic data storage media, and the reprinting of portions of text, are reserved	© 2017 novum publishing ISBN 978-3-99048-614-6 Editing: Nicola Ratcliff, BA Cover photo: Jerry Pearlman Cover design, layout & typesetting: novum publishing
Printed in the European Union on environmentally friendly, chlorine- and acid-free paper.	**www.novum-publishing.co.uk**

CONTENTS

Introduction	7
Dedication	8
Interpretation clause	9
Chapter 1 – The common attorney	10
Chapter 2 – Changes at the coal face – an overview	17
Chapter 3 – Conveyancing	36
Chapter 4 – Wills and probate	49
Chapter 5 – Licensing	55
Chapter 6 – Divorce and other marital matters	66
Chapter 7 – A criminal lawyer [or more accurately a criminal law practitioner]	80
Chapter 8 – Litigation	103
Chapter 9 – An uncommon common attorney	122
A miscellany	122
A miscellany of experiences	131
A miscellany of people	140
Chapter 10 – The dying embers but a spark of hope?	145
Chapter 11 – A nightmare scenario	169
Acknowlements	172

INTRODUCTION

It was intended to be an autobiography. I was recording how I remembered what life was like when I first entered the legal profession, over 50 years ago. But then I started to draw comparisons with how they are now. I was simply comparing the changes in practice, in a wonderful profession. As I went on, I realised that it was not only the practices that had changed, but the whole profession. Like others of my generation, I kept on saying 'we had the best days' and I firmly believe that. But as I read about the many changes which were occurring on an almost daily basis, I became convinced that the legal profession as I knew it, was dying, or at best that its very existence as a profession was at risk. I wondered whether the changes were in the public or any other interest and I thought about the famous man on the Clapham omnibus, perhaps now known to most, as Joe Public. Those thoughts are included at the end of most chapters. I realise, that even as I write, there are more and more changes being put into effect or being announced, so what I have written today may be very different within the next day or so.

I hope that I stimulate some debate and also that any reader has a good laugh about those 'old days'.

As it started out as an autobiography, I have included some of the stories that I like to tell, just so that they are not forgotten, even though, they are really just the ruminations of an old lawyer. On the other hand, I hope they demonstrate, that even a common attorney can have an incredibly varied and interesting career.

Jerry Pearlman
Leeds
2016

DEDICATION

– to –

My wife Bernice who has had to put up with my long winded sentences and poor spelling for over half a century

– and to –

The late Victor Zermansky
A fellow Leeds solicitor, competitor and friend who influenced my administrative skills, such as they are, and my professional standards

INTERPRETATION CLAUSE[1]

Words importing the masculine gender include the feminine.

Words importing the feminine gender include the masculine.

Words in the singular include the plural and words in the plural include the singular.

The Singular shall include the plural where appropriate and vice versa.

LSG shall mean the Law Society's Gazette.

Legal Aid shall be used where appropriate, to mean the newer Public Funding.

Divorce and Matrimonial shall be deemed to refer to Family.

The Common Attorney, the High Street Solicitor and Solicitor are used interchangeably. And sometimes, plain 'lawyer' is used for the sake of brevity.

---

1 As they say 'after the Section 6 Interpretation Act 1978'!

CHAPTER 1

THE COMMON ATTORNEY

What is 'an attorney'? Wikipedia says, that in England and Wales, it is a person, who may be, but is not necessarily, a lawyer, who is authorised to act on someone else's behalf, in either a business or a personal matter. Thus, we have a document called a Power of Attorney whereby, a person gives such an authority to another person, either generally or for some specific purpose. We also have the Attorney General, who is the person who is the principal legal advisor to the government and who sometimes represents the government in court, in particularly important cases.

Different types of legal practitioners were in existence as early as the thirteenth century, but their differences were eventually distinguished. It is said that the attorney performed whatever was not the exclusive functions of the barrister.[2] Attorneys were one of the so-called lower branches of the legal profession and they were the lawyers who had to cope with the intricacies of getting a case 'on its feet' and the barristers were the lawyers who argued the case in court. Actually, the attorneys were those who dealt with cases in the Common Law courts and the equivalent in the Chancery Courts were the solicitors. There was a third group of the lower branch, known as scriveners, who had a monopoly of conveyancing in the City of London. The titles were amalgamated by the Judicature Act 1872. There had been attempts to control the emerging profession and at one time, there was a Society of Gentleman Practitioners. They were all linked to the

---

2 The attorney in 18th Century England: Robson; Cambridge University Press. Footnote P4

Inns of Court but 'County Attorneys were ... exempt from the expenses of the Inn, save a small fee as 'out-members'.

By about 1450, the term 'solicitor' as used earlier, was recognised as meaning simply, one who 'urges, instigates, or conducts business on behalf of another person' and had come to mean one who concerned himself with legal business, but who was neither an attorney nor a barrister.[3]

An Act known by its reference 3 Jac I c7, was entitled 'to reform multitudes and misdemeanours of attorneys and solicitors at law'.

The term 'attorney' was in use in 1882 when W. S. Gilbert in Iolanthe had his Lord Chancellor sing:

I'll never assume that a rogue or a thief
Is a gentleman worthy implicit belief
Because his attorney has sent me a brief
(said I to myself – said I)

Towards the end of the nineteenth century, it was significant of this attitude that the respectable members of the profession were beginning to be known as solicitors, a term which, although less well established historically, had not habitually been coupled with the adjective 'pettifogging' as had the term attorney.[4] 'Pettifogging' as applied to a solicitor, has been defined as:

'... one who was not overscrupulous, and given to stirring up trouble in order that he would be employed to settle it'.[5]

One novelist claimed that by 1814 it could be said that there were no longer such things as attorneys in England.[6]

---

3 Ibid Footnote P4 Quoting Holdsworth 'History of English Law
4 Ibid P151
5 Ibid P137
6 Ibid

My favorite example of the use of the title is on a gravestone, in the churchyard at Askrigg in Wensleydale in Yorkshire, which describes the deceased gentleman, Mr. Myles Alderson, when he died in 1746, as 'An Honest Attorney' – but why this quality of honesty had to be singled out worries me. Was it so unusual?

I have taken a liberty and I have given the title of 'Common Attorney' to that type of lawyer who some call a 'high street lawyer'. And by this I mean a solicitor, more pompously formerly called 'a Solicitor of the Supreme Court'[7]. So although I may refer to the members of that other branch of the legal profession, namely 'the bar', whose members, known as barristers, are not publicans but lawyers, my focus is on the high street solicitor who was and sometimes still, is a self-confessed general practitioner – a jack of all trades. I will not continue by using the other part of that phrase namely 'a master of none' because many were, and I suppose that a few still are, genuinely men of all or most trades within the legal profession and are of great ability.

We may not have been the smartest kids on the block but we met with all sorts of people in all sorts of situations. We dealt with human misery, human success, human cupidity, human strengths and weaknesses – you say it and we have experienced it, all in a vicarious way. We were often able to synthesize several legal principles and apply them to the problem presented to us. The medical general practitioner was and perhaps still is, rather like that. I do not demean the medical profession but I do notice that now, some just feed the symptoms into the computer to work out what pill to prescribe and others are only too keen to refer you on to a consultant to have an x-ray or something else in the hospital. Yes, the legal profession has become something like that, but probably less so at high street level. I bow to no one in my admiration of those remaining country and market town solicitors who struggle in view of the changes that I will describe. But they are the exception and no longer the rule, and they are a dying breed.

---

7 Now known as a Solicitor of the Senior Court

It was the belief of the client, that the common attorney knew all the law (after all, ignorance of the law is no excuse!) and could give instant advice on any subject or problem raised with him. To the contrary, I learned whilst a student, that according to a marvelous handbook 'Learning the Law' by Glanville Williams[8], a good lawyer is not necessarily one who knows the law but is one who knows where to find the law.

Williams could not have been referring to the (I hope) fictional solicitor, who would say to a client "I must look that up in one of my text books" and would take from his shelves a large book with a leather binding embossed with something such as 'Burke's Law of England. Volume XIX' but inside the binding were pages headed 'Smiths A–Z guide to the Law.

'We were gentlemen!' So claimed Sir Thomas Lunn, the Secretary of the Law Society of England and Wales in the 1950s. (If he was around today, he would have been known as the CEO, the Chief Executive Officer.) He claimed that by some long forgotten statute, we were entitled to use the word 'Esquire' after our names. When I read in the Law Society's Gazette in 2012, that the haulage company, Eddie Stobbart, was planning to open 1300 law offices, my first thought was, how the mighty have fallen. It was not in an edition of the Gazette published on the 1st of April, so it was not an April Fool's Day joke. It was well known that the Co-op and Tesco were planning to enter the fray. It was as though they looked upon the law as an industry, but when it was part of a haulage empire, it just seemed to me, to be a leap too far, but it was not. The next step down into the abyss is that a firm of what used to be called 'bookies' (Betfair) has announced that it is offering a fixed-fee legal service to small and medium sized businesses and start ups.

Lawyers have never been the favorite of advisers, even in ancient times. Plato apparently, maliciously said:

---

8 Pub. Sweet and Maxwell

'The lawyer has learned how to flatter his master in word and indulge him in deed; but his soul is small and unrighteous ... from the first he has practiced deception and retaliation, and has become stunted and warped. And so he has passed out of youth into manhood, having no soundness in him.'

Even the bard could not resist a dig at us 'The first thing we do, let's kill all the lawyers'.[9] Another view was that of John Gay the poet:

I know you lawyers can, with ease,
Twist words and meanings as you please
That language, by your skill made pliant,
Will bend to favour ev'ry client.

And Boswell reports that Samuel Johnson said 'he did not speak ill of any man behind his back but he believed that the gentleman was an attorney'![10]

On the other hand we were one of the three great professions, in the eyes of the thinking classes – the church, the law and the army. I rather like the description by one writer:

'There is something by which a lawyer can be instantly recognised ... and by which lawyers, however dissimilar otherwise, are more clearly linked than they are separated by their differences ... A man who had a legal training is never quite the same again ... And ... is never able to look at institutions or administrative practices or even social and political policies free from his legal habits or belief.'[11]

---

9 Henry VI, Part 2. Act 4 Sc 2 line 2384
10 Boswell: Life of Johnson
11 Griffith: The Law of Property in Law and Opinion in England in the 20th Century

It took a long time before solicitors in particular and their trade union or representative organization, the Law Society, felt that they should do something about their image. I was one of the first public relations officers who was appointed to speak on behalf of the profession, locally. We had a local television station and I was a regular attender at their studios, to give my thoughts on any number of issues. I saw myself as someone who was there to defend the profession as well as assist the public, by giving them information about the law. I do not know if I succeeded. I well recollect one spin off from the new approach. The National Law Society held a conference to inform us of how we should go about our work. I remember little about that part of the weekend. What I do remember, is the keynote speaker. It was Enoch Powell and both my wife and I assumed that we would listen to him with great hostility. In fact, he was one of the best speakers that I have ever had the pleasure to hear. What a pity he blotted his copy book.

Many years later, I realised that we still had not made much progress in making us more media friendly. I learned that dentists had suddenly started adopting the title 'Doctor'. So I eventually came up with the idea that solicitors should also adopt the title 'Dr'. In Germany a lawyer is Herr Doktor, in France a lawyer attracts the title 'Maitre'. I learnt that in Canada, lawyers had decided to call themselves Doctor. All my efforts were unsuccessful. I wrote to the Law Society's Gazette but several solicitors who had a doctorate awarded by a university, felt that their status was being diminished. Perhaps I will return to this campaign at some time in the future

So to reflect upon the changes. No, I am not a Luddite but the changes have gone too far. On the other hand, I could say that I am fast becoming a Luddite myself, because I am having so much trouble keeping up with modern developments. Of course it will be said, that anyone who resists the type of change that is taking place, is doing so for personal and financial reasons. But in the field of law, in the end, it is the client or the public who will gain or suffer. It is not only the commerciality of change.

It is also the changes within the law, the procedures, the people and the standards. It is about the diminishing protection for people. There are some who manage to receive more than their fair share of legal help, usually the very rich. Others, those with limited means, are deprived of what was looked upon by the old timers as being the reason for the legal profession existing, are now denied help.

When I was in my very early days as a practitioner, I met a man in a bar. He was a solicitor – not a barrister – and he did not tell me a shaggy dog story. In fact, he passed on to me, one of the more sage pieces of advice that I ever received. After hearing of my aspirations, which were to build up a practice, he said "don't forget the widow's mite." He went on to explain that you might be having a meeting with a wealthy client, claiming thousands or hundreds of thousands of pounds and the next client may be a widow worried about a problem which involved ten pounds. Her problem was as serious and worrying to her, as the wealthy man with his thousands. That was the widow's mite. You had to give as much of your professional expertise to the widow, as you did to the wealthy businessman. That was professionalism. You were not motivated simply by profit or time, but there must be an element of humanitarianism. Years later, I was at a farewell party for a commercial lawyer who was moving firms. I asked him about the satisfaction that he expected to get from his work and I mentioned that my greatest satisfaction, was when I had helped an individual who was in trouble and I was able to do something which made that person's life bearable. The departing lawyer responded "I want to do deals. I want to do deals." Clearly, people and their problems were of no concern to him. I doubt if he ever had as much satisfaction from his work as I had from mine.

Later, when I start to examine some parts of legal practice, I will tell you about some of my experiences and I hope that you will find some to be salacious, some surprising, some amusing and some, which illustrate the best and worst of legal practice and the great wide world of the high street solicitor or common attorney.

CHAPTER 2

CHANGES AT THE COAL FACE – AN OVERVIEW

> In serving writs I made such a name
> That an articled clerk I soon became:
> I wore clean collars and a brand new suit
> For the pass examination at the Institute
> And that pass examination did so well for me,
> That I am now the Ruler of the Queen's Navee!
>
> H.M.S Pinafore. Act 1

In my first few weeks as an articled clerk (now called a trainee solicitor) my principal, somewhat generously, enabled me to go up to the North East of England where my parents then lived. We had a client buying a house and as the vendor's solicitors were in Newcastle, I could go to complete the transaction (more about 'completions' later). I went up by bus and after visiting my parents, went to the office in Newcastle-upon-Tyne. It was, and still is, a very old established and prestigious firm. As I waited to move from reception to a room where we were to carry out the transaction, I noticed that they still made the copies of letters using a letter press. To this day, I have never really known how they work but it involves purple dye and pressing the actual letter against a piece of copy paper and the words are copied. Before moving on, I should mention that many years later, I took my children to the Industrial Museum at Beamish and found a room which was a pastiche of an old time solicitor's office and there, I found that same letter press, accompanied by an acknowledgement to the firm that I had visited.

Typewriters and carbon paper were par for the course. So was shorthand and one dictated letters and documents to a shorthand typist who duly transcribed them. When I had enough work to justify employing a secretary, I found that at first, I could type faster than her. She was one of the very, very best secretaries that I ever had and soon she was quicker, much quicker, than me. Eventually, she became one of the fastest typists in the city. I say that, because eventually, she moved to work for one of the top officers of the City Council and I learned about her prestigious status from someone in the Civic Hall.

It was a waste of time, when taking a statement from a witness, to have your secretary sitting there waiting for you to ask the question, as sometimes, especially so with a client in a criminal case, they might have been making it up as they went along. So at first, I used to write out the statement by hand and then have it typed up. I found this so boring and often lost concentration. I had heard about methods of voice recording and I bought a huge Uher reel to reel tape recorder. This revolutionized my whole life. I could deal with several matters at a time and whilst I was dictating, my secretary was already typing.

If you wanted to include a plan in a document, it had to be copied by hand. If you wanted to send someone a copy of a letter or a document, it had to be typed out in full (other than Abstracts of Title about which more later). It was painfully slow. Then came the first copying machines. They were large and cumbersome. You poured different chemicals into various parts of the machine and copied and first photographed and then developed the image. It took time and also you had to empty the machine after you had finished using it for the day. Then there was invented, the electrostatic copying machine, or what we still tend to refer to, as the Xerox. It was and still is, just wonderful and saves so much time. How did we ever manage without it?

Of course we had telephones and eventually, as we had some international commercial clients, we acquired a telex machine. I was at a lunch once and was sitting next to a partner in a big commercial firm and he 'put me down' by telling me that they had a fax machine and that the new machines had limitations as well as benefits. He had finished a long and complex document that morning and sent it by fax to the solicitor 'on the other side'. Within two hours, it came back with all the amendments suggested by that other solicitor. I realised that we would be out of the race if we did not get one, so we did.

Our first word processor was a huge machine that cost £10,000. We had spent six months mulling over whether we needed it or could afford it. Actually, I doubt whether we saved enough in terms of time because it took quite a long time before we really understood the ways in which we could use it to its best advantage. Now you can buy a perfectly satisfactory PC or personal computer for under £500.

They were the days of the managing clerk, who was usually a man without any formal qualifications, who may have started as the office boy and learned his trade as he worked his way through the office. He may have been the conveyancing clerk or even the litigation clerk. They were the salt of the earth and many of them were marvelous characters. I remember one in a firm in which I worked, who was a snuff user and his waistcoat – he appeared to have only one – which was never changed or washed – was littered with the droppings of his snorting. They are now formalised as Legal Executives.

I have always presumed, that amongst the reasons which cause the dislike or fear of lawyers, is the fact that we are alleged to twist people's words, but mainly the reason is, that we charge for our services. If you listen closely to the manner in which a good advocate applies logic to the statement of a witness, or the presentation of an argument, as to the manner in which the law should be applied to a given set of facts, you must surely acknowledge that it is an art and not a mystery. I sat in the House of Lords (that part of the House which was the most senior court of appeal in the Nation, which has been replaced by the Supreme Court) with two non-lawyers and as they, and I, listened to the skilled arguments, all of us recognised the pure brilliance of a good advocate doing his job.

The issue of charging for one's services has bedeviled the legal profession. It is one of the few issues where it must be unequivocally acknowledged that the changes have been beneficial. There was a time when, if there were not set fees for a particular service, such as conveyancing (the transfer of land and buildings), it was quite normal for a solicitor to say to himself "How much is it worth?" He might hold the file in his hand and 'get a feel' of it and fix a fee in that arbitrary manner. Then some more realistic principles were introduced and the fees which one could charge, were to be established by the time spent on the job. Eventually, judges recognized that sometimes, a particular element of the matter justified the introduction of an additional factor. This was the 'adrenalin factor'. The judge said that a lawyer would be struggling with a particularly difficult matter and would be thinking about it in his bath. If it was that type of case, it justified a higher fee. Now everything is 'time based'. Each lawyer sets his 'charging rate' according to his level of experience or expertise. He decides whether the market will accept that rate and he records the time spent on behalf of the client, usually in ten minute segments, then enters it into some form of record, whether computer or manually based, and calculates his fee accordingly.

I had a client [A] who instructed me that he had a very good deal. He could buy a garage business and property at a bargain price of £10,000, but the transaction had to be completed in two days. I agreed, that subject to certain qualifications, it was just possible. I asked the identity of the vendors' solicitors and was told that I had to phone the vendors who would supply the details. I phoned and heard one man [B] call another to the phone and then I heard the voice of [C]. I recognised the voices because I was then currently defending C on a fraud charge. I realised the deal was certainly an attempted fraud on my client, A. I described the fraudster C and asked A if the vendor fitted that description. It did and A's interest died. I had saved him £10,000. I sent him a bill for two Guineas (£2.2s.0d. or £2.10p in new money). He complained to me saying that it was too expensive, because I was wanting to be paid two guineas for one phone call. I was so annoyed that I refused to act for A again.

Now the emphasis is on the use of first names and I still cringe when the office girl calls me 'Jerry'. I do like some formality and prefer to be called 'Mr. Pearlman' by most people, other than social contacts and others who know me well. In my first few years I had dealings with a stockbroker and it was a fairly informal relationship. He was my predecessor as an officer of a charity. I was upset that he always called me 'Pearlman'. I thought that he was being stand-offish until I was told that it was in fact, one step nearer to actual friendship. I never met anyone else who used the absence of a title in that way. In fact, in school and in the army, it was a manner of showing your superiority to 'Smith'. All others were 'sir' or were your equivalent and you used their first name.

Dress is now fairly informal. You see many people in a business or professional situation who do not wear a tie, sometimes even with a business suit. Solicitors in court are expected to wear a jacket, preferably a suit jacket, but you see many now wearing a blazer and tie. A tie is needed and I cannot remember seeing a solicitor appearing in court without a tie.

There was a rather pompous county court judge in Bradford, who caused a notice to the following effect to be displayed in the solicitors robing room:

> 'His Honour has noted that several solicitors are appearing before him without a waistcoat. Solicitors are requested that if they do not wear a waistcoat they should keep their jackets closed whilst in court'.

We are also criticised because of our use of language. Too many words; too many long words; too much Latin; too much gobbledygook. At one time, we were paid by the number of words that we used in a document. This was by folio which was 72 words.

To me, there are some standard phrases which roll off the tongue, which I feel, are beautiful in their own right. My favorite is:

> 'IN WITNESS whereof the parties hereto have hereunto set their hands and seals the day and year first hereinbefore written'

Beautiful, isn't it? Better than 'We signed it today'!

At one time, one could not even enroll for a law course, or even become articled (today it is called a training contract) unless you had passed Latin at school certificate or 'highers'. More about articles later. It was not so much that you would use Latin as a language in your work, but it has the beauty and the succinctness of such phrases as-

Nemo dat quod non habet [No one gives what he does not possess]

Volenti non fit injuria [That to which a man consents cannot be considered an injury]

Res ipsa loquitur [The thing speaks for itself]

Fi. Fa. The abbreviation for *Fieri Facias* [the form of Order to a bailiff to levy execution – not to take off his head but to seize goods of a debtor to be sold to pay off a debt or judgment]

Res judicata [A thing adjudicated upon]

Or my favorite *Omnia praesumuntur rite et solemniter esse acta* [All things are presumed correctly and solemnly done].

We even have some throwbacks from the days when legal French was used such as market *ouvert* [Goods bought in certain open markets transferred title even though they had been stolen]

Perhaps they were introduced so that the draftsman did not achieve his 72 words?

Even the distinction between solicitor and barrister is becoming blurred. They are still different professions or different sub-categories of the same profession. One is controlled by Statute (the Solicitors Acts) and the other by common law. One is controlled by the Solicitor's Regulation Authority, the independent regulatory body of the Law Society of England and Wales and the other by the Inns of Court and by the Bar Council. One was traditionally, the profession of the rich and the other, the job for the less rich. One was the profession of great advocates and the other, prepared the cases for them. One got the credit for winning great jury trials and the other, hid behind their robes. One were bewigged and the other bare headed. One supplied the judges and the other the minor judicial functionaries. One was rich and the other often fabulously rich. In each pair guess which is which!

There was a Q.C. who became the Stipendiary Magistrate of Leeds, who refused to even meet the client who was accused of murder, on the basis that they might become emotionally involved.[12]

I instructed Sir John Foster Q.C. in a case in Uganda sorting out an argument between two kingdom-native tribes. As we went to the hearing in a car from Entebbe to Kampala, John sat in the front and I and the two junior barristers, were squeezed together in the back. At one stage, John turned round and said 'I am one of those silks (Q.C.s) who does not mind being spoken to during the course of a case'!!

Barristers were not allowed to entertain solicitors, even to take them out for lunch. Fortunately, some managed to escape the restriction, but not publicly, only in their homes.

We eventually established some sort of equality on the North Eastern Circuit, in that, we had a joint garden party each year for the Lawyers Benevolent Association. I mentioned to the bar representative, that I had heard that in London solicitors were being invited to Bar Mess.[13] I suggested that the North Eastern Bar should do the same and also, that they should invite the Presidents of the Local Law Societies, of which, I was one. He denied that any such arrangement existed or could ever be possible. A few weeks later, I was sitting next to the Lord Chief Justice, at a dinner and raised the issue with him. He agreed that it was happening in London and should happen in our area. Thereafter, I mentioned it to successive leaders of the Circuit, over about ten years and was given promises that never materialised until the late Brian Walsh Q.C. was the leader and he succeeded where oth-

---

12 'Most of my murders'. E. John Parris
13 Barristers have an elite dinning club. They meet once a month sometimes with the resident or visiting judges. On my circuit they had a renowned cellar of wonderful vintages. They also had a collection of silver because a visiting barrister was expected to show appreciation to his hosts by a presentation of silver.

ers failed. Although I had been out of the chair for many years ('There is nothing so past as a past president') I was invited. I hope that the practice still continues.

Nowadays, many commercial law solicitors earn the big fees and a rather small number of barristers get the high profile big fee cases. There are solicitor judges even in the High Court (but still a disproportionately small number of them). It is quite usual to see solicitors and barristers and their respective families dining out together and even going on holiday together. There are solicitor advocates in the High Court and many in the Crown Courts – in fact, the junior bar is suffering from the fact that there is not enough work for them. Barristers do not always wear wigs, especially in the higher courts, so sometimes, they are indistinguishable from solicitors.

A solicitor is always pleased to claim that he gave a successful barrister his first brief, but it is strange that although barristers are actually beholden to solicitors for their work, once the barrister becomes established, he becomes arrogant and dismissive of his solicitor and his work. I had a barrister stay with me on a sort of boys weekend. He eventually asked for time to read his papers for a case the next day. He told me that as a matter of course, he did not read the brief from any solicitor, because they were always rubbish. All that he did, was to read the prosecution papers, the statement of the accused (the 'proof of evidence' or just the 'proof') and work out the defence from there.

Sometimes, when a barrister becomes a judge he does not necessarily forget the solicitors who gave him work. I had a case in the High Court with three parties, each represented by a Q.C. We all turned up to start the case and were kept waiting for almost half an hour. The judge was a chap whom I had instructed on a regular basis, when he was still just a barrister and we always had got on well. He came into court and as he sat down, he said (looking in my direction) "I can't hear this case. I know your instructing solicitor." My Q.C. said "Excuse me, my lord. Are you asking us or telling us?" "I am telling you." he replied and went on "I will get my clerk to find you another judge."

And that was it for the day. I told this story to some Circuit (i.e. more local) Judges and they all said, that if they applied such a rule, they would never hear a case, because they had been instructed by many of the solicitors whose cases came before them.

It can be even worse. I regularly instructed one particular barrister (I shall call him Mr. X because, although I admire his skills, I feel so aggrieved by some of his conduct towards me, that I must avoid him suggesting that I have defamed him – I shall plead justification) – because he was even more expert than me in a very specialist subject. I was instructed by a London Borough in a case, somehow related to the site of The Dome – now the O2 Centre. I, in turn, instructed the said Mr. X. As the advice turned to action, I realised that nothing was happening and I then learned that Mr. X had said to the Borough Solicitor "I can't understand why you are instructing a solicitor in Leeds when you have a quite competent legal department of your own." I never heard from the Borough again. That's thanks for you. Then he committed the opposite sin. We were in a car going to a site visit and I mentioned to him that I was dealing with a case, but was having difficulty in obtaining legal aid. A week later I learned that he had seen a letter from my client and he had replied recommending that my client should approach a firm of solicitors in another city. When I complained to X, he who never seemed to forget anything, apologised, saying that he had not remembered our conversation in the car and never connected the two. I have letters of apology from him relating to both matters.

Even so, I believe in the separation of functions between solicitor and barrister. Sometimes it may cost the client a little more and sometimes the solicitor could have done better without the barrister, but overall I feel that there is strength in their joint enterprise and most clients benefit from it.

One reason for the public attitude to barristers, is caused by what was the rule that, apart from a few exceptions, a member of the public could not approach or instruct a barrister directly. He had to do so through a solicitor. This resulted in the barrister standing somewhat apart from his lay client. To the client, the barrister seemed remote, rather aloof and, of course bewigged. To the barrister, it meant that as that stipendiary magistrates said, he did not get emotionally involved. Neither did the barrister pick up the baggage, both physically and emotionally. At the end of a case, the barrister hands his papers to the solicitor and stalks off. The solicitor is left with the client either complaining or enquiring about what his rights are now that he has won or lost. The barrister rarely bothers to find out what happened next. I recall one case, when I had to more or less drag the barrister to the cells to sympathise with our client who had hoped that he would walk free, but was on his way to prison.

That was the barrister who was selected by the client – not by me. Apparently he had secured an acquittal for him in a minor motoring charge some years earlier. I knew that the barrister was very clever and had an incredible ability to absorb the detail of a case in a short period of time. It was said that he could rise early and absorb a difficult brief before breakfast. To avoid any problems, I delivered the brief early and insisted on a conference a few weeks before the hearing. The fee just for the conference was over £600! It was likely to be a guilty plea but if so advised, then the presentation of a weighty mitigation. As we entered the room, the barrister was flicking through the papers and after a short chat said 'I think that this is a case where we play the man and not the ball' and he went on to ask the client questions about himself, which were already in the brief. I realised that he had not read the brief except as we sat there. At the end, as he was ushering us out of the room, he said to me "We must discuss that other case." There was no other case. As soon as he closed the door he said "Jerry – you'll never guess where I was 24 hours ago." "No." "I was water skiing on the South China Seas." I quickly worked out that he could not have arrived back in town until about 15 minutes before the conference. He earned that fee easily!

I have complained that there are few solicitors who become High Court judges. I made that point in my Presidential Address when I presided over the formal dinner of my local Law Society. Mention of my speech was made in the Gazette and of course there were letters from those who were satisfied with the lower level appointments which they had been granted. I was concerned because three of the four solicitors who I knew well, who had been granted temporary judicial posts, had found that the appointments were not renewed. I noticed that from time to time, one did read of solicitor appointments as circuit judges or the very occasional High Court judge but I realize that it was another of my campaigns that I lost.

According to the Gazette website[14]:

> 'Solicitors stand no better a chance of being recommended as a judge than they did eight years ago, new figures prove. Statistics released by the Judicial Appointments Commission show a third of recommendations for the 87 deputy district judge posts in 2014 were for solicitors, even though solicitors made up 58% of the 1,114 applications,'

Well, you can't win 'em all.

A reader will conclude that I have problems with the other branch of our profession. I will admit to having a love/hate relationship with that other branch. I admire their skills and many of them are quite brilliant. I owe them a great debt because to a certain extent the solicitor succeeds on the back of the good barrister. But there is something about them as a group which has caused me problems. So many of them become – well, I will say it – arrogant. Not all I admit, but I have observed them in and out of court and I suggest that the very formal way in which they have to conduct themselves in court before the judges leads to them becoming very formal, stiff and conceited men (and it is mainly the men, some will be pleased to learn!)

Having vented my spleen, I add that I feel that Joe Public is likely to be worse off, if that branch dies or is severely wounded. Their skills do much to preserve the rule of law.

---

14 5 June 2015

How sad it was to read in the Times[15] that they were accused of paying 'backhanders' to solicitors to obtain work. 'How are the mighty humbled'? The Times reported:

> 'A thriving black market in 'backhanders' paid by barristers to solicitors to secure cases is to be outlawed in a drive to raise standards in criminal trials … recent curbs on legal aid fees have led to an increase in the practice.

An aspiring solicitor had to enter into 'articles of clerkship' – now called a training contract. It was usual for the 'employer' to receive a premium, in my case it was £500 which my parents could hardly afford. I did not start by enrolling at a University to take a degree, so my articles were for a period of five years, which ought to have been five years hard labour. Instead I had an easy time, because my principal left my tuition to his managing clerk who did not mind when I turned up. I arrived late for work and then had a long lunch in the university 'caf'. One had to attend classes at a University for a couple of days a week for a year, known as the statutory year.

It was a profession to aspire to, because you were almost certain to have a secure future. You would be seen as a solid citizen. You would be trusted. You would make a good living. You were there to advise and to help. That word 'help' was the word that I felt was most important if I was to fulfill my aspirations.

I do not remember worrying about liability or responsibility when I started. I may have had an indemnity insurance policy in case I 'boobed' and left myself open to a claim for compensation. Perhaps I did arrange insurance then but if I did not, then I am sure that I soon did arrange a policy. I never remember having any problem about being able to afford the premium but now it is a major financial expense. I see from my early accounts that I only had to spend £48 on all insurance. I under-

---

15 1 October 2015

stand that £20,000 per annum per solicitor or partner is now the going rate for an indemnity policy, for a practitioner with a good claims record. There are insurers who are themselves, unable to pay the amount of the compensation, and there are solicitors who because of their past mistakes, are unable to obtain cover. Sensibly, it is now a requirement of being granted your practicing certificate (the permission to practise which also attracts a fee of £1000) that you have indemnity insurance and it follows, that if you do not have such insurance, you cannot continue as a solicitor. I have been consulted, as a senior practitioner, by such a worried practitioner who had a confused relationship with his insurers and who was only offered cover on such a high premium that he had to cease practice.

I clearly learned a lesson from the Glanville Williams phrase that I have quoted. During my first year in practice, when a travelling salesman from one of the law publishers, called into my office, he had no difficulty in convincing me that I had to buy a good library. He made it easy by offering me the chance to buy it by installments, I bought the whole package which I remember as:
- Halsbury's Laws of England
- Halsbury's Statutes
- The Encyclopedia of Forms and Precedents
- The Encyclopedia of Court Forms and Precedents
- A subscription to the All England Law Reports
- Rules of Court [the White Book]
- [Later] Current Law

My accounts show that all I spent on books that year was £63. I found that they impressed my clients and proved to be absolutely essential. In addition, I used them as a learning and teaching aide. I tried, as I developed my practice, to keep abreast of various types of legal practice. In the two encyclopedias you can find, grouped in sections, a wonderful variety of documents, which can be the basis of most transactions. Whenever I turned to the books for the precedent of a particular document, I would ensure that I also read the previous two or three precedents and the next two or three. In this way, I learned about many types of transactions which I never knew existed but gave me some understanding of how I might go about a job if ever asked to do so. I hardly ever had cause to use any of them ... but you never know. I used to advise my articled clerks to follow my practice. I could tell which were going to go on to be good practitioners. They were the ones who took my advice.

Now these books can still be bought in hardback, but a practitioner who chooses to have them is more likely to buy them online, at a slightly lower price. I understand that even then, the cost is likely to be:

- Halsbury's Laws of England – £10605
- Halsbury's Statutes – I have not been able to discover the price but based on the rest it is likely to be in the region of £8000
- The Encyclopedia of Forms and Precedents – £10394
- The Encyclopedia of Court Forms and Precedents [Atkins] – £8151 [yes £8151 plus £534 per annum for the up dated loose leaf service]
- A subscription to the All England Law Reports – £829 per annum[16]
- Rules of the Supreme Court [the White Book] £630

Amongst the principles that distinguished us from traders, were either that we could not advertise and we could not share the fees, with anyone who was not qualified. It is the changes to these two principles, in particular, which I find the hardest with which to come to terms. When I see the nature and extent of advertising, whether in newspapers, on television or on the back of buses, I feel uncomfortable. I do not know how I would decide whether I would advertise if I was now dependent on finding new clients. It might be a necessity but it would cause me some pain.

---

16 Prices kindly supplied by Butterworths

The introduction of the Alternative Business Structure[17] is really the concept of business and not profession. Once again, I would feel uncomfortable but it might be the only way to survive. I accept that each of them could be of some benefit to Joe Public but they are only of benefit to the Common Attorney if it keeps him in business. Once he goes down either of those routes he is losing the true essence of professionalism.

The concept of sharing fees has been overridden in so many ways that it was with surprise that I read recently, that there was to be restriction. The concept of alternative business structures, which I explain later, is the antithesis of this principle. The second is summed up by a colleague who commented to me:

> In your day your clients were proud to say "we must use Mr Pearlman again" when they came to move. You will have acted for them and their friends and families for years. You have built up a relationship with them as the family solicitor. That loyalty is now strained to breaking point. So far as the first time buyers or those with no affinity to a particular solicitor are concerned; they are unlikely to get anywhere near the traditional average high street firm. The power brokers are the estate agents particularly the well known estate agency chains. They are selling services not just houses. These powerful corporates have renounced the practice of referring their clients to their favourite local solicitor who provided a friendly professional and personal service for nothing more than a bottle of wine at Christmas. Their staff are expected to channel the seller and the buyer to panel firms en masse, for significant referral fees. The majority of buyers will go along with the

---

17 A structure where a non-lawyer enters into an arrangement with a solicitor where they run a business – note 'business' not 'profession' – and carry out many types of legal work as long as a qualified solicitor is in some way involved

agents "friendly" recommendation. Why shouldn't they? This is a significant source of revenue to the agent. Is this in the public interest?'

But I was astonished by the revelation of the Lord Chancellor, Michael Gove, who announced that he was going to take action on breaches of the banned practice of paying referral fees in criminal cases. He rightly said:

> "This not something I will tolerate. Work should go to the advocate most qualified for the job, not to the highest bidder."[18]

We were either sole practitioners or were in partnerships. Now one can limit liability by being a limited company or a limited liability partnership. I never heard of a solicitor being made bankrupt, unless he had had his hand in the till but now there are any number of bankruptcies or other forms of insolvency.

The first step one now takes, when acquiring a new client, is to address issues such as, money laundering and proof of identity. Then you send out a client engagement letter with T & Cs – Terms and Conditions – sounds like buying on the Internet!

There is one principle that continues and which does mark us out as a profession. It is the binding undertaking. It is akin to saying 'my word is my bond'. If a solicitor says 'I will undertake to do this' he must do it. It is a practice that enables some transactions to proceed. When the seller's solicitor receives the sale price for the property, which was mortgaged to a lender, the seller's solicitor undertakes to pay off the mortgage, out of the money that he has received. It is accepted by all parties that he will deal with it as he promised. Sometimes, when some action must be taken in the conduct of a case through the courts, a solicitor will give an undertaking to the judge, that he will, for instance,

---

18 LSG 13 July 2015

file a document within a given period of time. The court will accept that it will be done. Why are undertakings of such importance to the solicitor and to Joe Public? It is because failure to honour an undertaking will almost certainly lead to the solicitor being struck off the roll[19].

To be struck off the roll, means the end of your career and thus, the organisation which oversees our conduct is the Solicitors Conduct Authority, which is a fearsome body to us. When I first entered practice, it was the Law Society which dealt with all matters relating to us and this included disciplinary matters. Now they have been hived off to an independent body, but I still have a slight tremor when I hear from the Law Society. It is rather like seeing a police car as you drive, even if you have been observing the speed limit during the whole of your journey.

The Law Society is now the helper to the solicitor. It is really our trade union, but is much more than that. It maintains standards and is the font of control of every aspect of a solicitor's professional existence. It is the organisation which gives us professional status and is looked upon by politicians and the public alike, as the embodiment of the profession of solicitors. Although the two functions are separate, they are still looked upon by many solicitors as being departments of the same organisation.

For the High Street solicitor, one of the overriding problems is that of the restriction upon the availability of state funding, originally known as 'Legal Aid and Advice' but now 'Public Funding'. That is a theme of much as what follows.

I have claimed in one place that I am not a Luddite, but then I contradict myself by criticising some changes or the pace of change. I have managed to cope with some of the emerging technology, but I fear that little by little, it is advancing at a faster pace than I can cope with.

---

19 There is a list of all solicitors called the Roll. When one qualifies it is said that you are admitted to the Roll and the person in legal control is the Master of the Rolls, one of the most senior of High Court judges.

I would guess that there is not a solicitor, who is not computer literate. Computer literacy is recognised as being at the root of being able to practise as an attorney of any sort. The well-known author, Richard Susskind, believes that technology is the driving force involved in the changes in the legal profession. Whether it can go as far as so-called cloud computing (because of confidentiality issues), the use of packaged documents, video conferencing or because of the threat from Alternative Business Structures, are matters with which my successors will have to struggle.

I cope less well with the many changes in the procedures involved in practicing, in almost every field of law with which a Common Attorney is likely to deal. However, all this has to be seen in a wider context, which can be summed up by posing three questions, as I look at the changes that I have observed.

They are:

Firstly – are we now a trade and no longer a profession? Is it work for a professional person? By profession, I mean as one of the three vocations[20]. By trade I imply an emphasis on commerce so that it is simply a financial transaction.

Secondly – 'Is it good for the common attorney?'

But even more pertinent, thirdly – 'Is it good for Joe Public?'

I do not claim to have a definite answer to those questions. It is rather like the man who was heard to say that he was looking for a one handed lawyer and when asked to explain, he said that he was tired of asking his lawyer a question and being told that "On the one hand yes, but on the other hand no."

I see some advantages in various parts of the work and practices of the modern solicitor but I feel that there are significant disadvantages. I shall point out some of them but each solicitor, each client and each reader will have a different view. I will give my view of some of the advantages brought about by some of the changes but I know that it is not the lawyers, but the great British public, Mr. Joe Public, who will decide. In some cases, they

---

20 The three vocations are the church, medicine and the law.

will vote with their feet and choose to use the new people who offer a competitive service, but who I consider to be interlopers.

I also try and record some of those practices and, as far as I am able, to tell you about some replacement practices. However, I must admit that I am not up to date with all the changes. Some are actually beyond my knowledge or understanding.

And I believe that many changes have been introduced with the best of intentions. Nevertheless, it is true to say that the old adage that 'hard cases make bad law' can apply to legislation as well as case law. The other well-known phrase is about 'unintended consequences'. I suspect, that many of the changes that have been brought about have been introduced because of a perceived bad practice which has been disadvantageous to some member of the public. But in their haste to stop any so-called malpractice, the government has often gone over the top and caused problems that it did not even expect. It will be up to you, the reader, to decide whether or not I have are identified cases where there have been these unintended consequences and consequent unfairness.

It was summed up by a young lady solicitor who wrote in the Law Society's Gazette[21] 'Nowadays when I say I am a lawyer I often get the reaction 'are you lot extinct?!'

Many years ago, the profession was treated with respect but the legal sector has been commoditised. There are downsides to this but we are now more accessible and more approachable. So it's swings and roundabouts.

---

21 17th March 2014

CHAPTER 3

CONVEYANCING

If there is any subject, any branch of law or legal practice that brings opprobrium on the heads of solicitors it is this. And once we had a monopoly.

Conveyancing is the process of transferring the ownership of land and any buildings on it from the seller to the buyer. It is done by a written document. Originally, it was known as an Indenture because it was prepared in duplicate, on one big piece of parchment and the two copies cut apart by a wavy line so that the place of separation was 'in and out' namely indented, thus indentures. Apprentices were 'indentured' for a similar reason. Their agreement with their master was prepared in duplicate, in the same way and similarly cut, so that each party had a copy.

You can still see these documents but they are more than likely to be the framed artifacts hanging in a pub so as to give the image of age and history, or they are parts of light shades. It does not matter what they say but they are still an object of beauty. They were written in old English script with certain words or phrases, traditionally in capitals or coloured. Just to hold the parchment gives one a feeling of importance and permanency. Whilst every so often it may be necessary to look at them, to clarify some point about a particular property, they are very much an artifact of the past although the methods of making them are preserved for such documents as illuminated addresses.

Only qualified lawyers could carry out the procedure of conveyancing. In fact it was a criminal offence to prepare a deed unless you were amongst the privileged classes. And with good cause.

My main type of property transaction was the small house so common in my city – some were built back to back and were so named. They cost about £500 on average and I used to say that

I would not buy a car that cost more than the cost of the average house that I conveyed. The houses, or such of them as are left, now sell for as much as £150,000 but you can get a good car for £20,000. There were fixed fees for the transaction according to the purchase price.

I regularly instructed a young and upcoming barrister and I now think that he did not want one of his solicitors to think that he had instructed another to help him buy a house so he decided to do it himself. I received an agonised phone call from him one Saturday morning. He had started the procedure himself. He was obtaining a mortgage from a Building Society and it had instructed its own solicitors to look after their interests. As they viewed the written title they discovered a fault. To be technical, the previous owners had bought the property, in such a way, that they held it in what was known as a strict settlement, as opposed to the more usual arrangement, which was as a trust for sale[22]. It was probably going to be an enormous job to unscramble the mess. He wanted to know what to do. I came up with the idea that as the likelihood of there being a real problem in the future was remote he should pay for title insurance. He did so, I took over and he had his house. I did notice that later, when he moved house, he did not ask me for help. By that time he was probably sufficiently eminent that he could use one of the big firms who were now his clients so he did not need to worry if I, still a small practitioner, felt abandoned.

In the days before photocopiers you had to provide copies of the documents which proved the Vendor's ownership to the property [the title]. There was a very peculiar manner of pro-

---

22 A Trust for sale is the usual manner in law in which two or more persons own a property. It is to be contrasted with a tenancy in common. When two or more people own a property jointly as joint tenants then on the death of one of them the interest of the deceased accrues to the survivor. When it a tenancy in common the share of the deceased passes according to his will.

viding the copy called an Abstract of Title. A skilled legal secretary knew how to use shortened versions of some common words (rather like texting today) and other parts of the summary were assigned particular margins so a regular reader knew exactly where to look for a particular piece of information.

The purchaser's solicitor would, and still does, make enquires of the local authorities, using some standard forms called the local search. He then asks the vendor's solicitors some questions about the property, the Enquiries before Contract, and about other matters which were known to the vendor. All this was fairly brief. Contracts were then physically exchanged and a deposit paid. The purchaser's solicitor then drafted the conveyance, which was approved by the vendor's solicitor and a fair copy then typed on heavy paper, although by now, it was not on real parchment but an imitation. Some words had to be in capitals and the deed ended with the lovely sentence starting 'IN WITNESS whereof etc.' that I have already quoted. Completion took place at the Vendor's solicitor's office by the handing over of a bank draft in exchange for the title deeds including the conveyance and the keys of the house, if there was a house. This was a more modern procedure because at one time, as the completion was not necessarily on the land, it was usual for a sod of earth to be 'delivered' – thus the '*deliver*' in 'signed sealed and *delivered*'.

Completion was an important event because not only did it get you out of the office, but more importantly, you were able to get some impression of how busy the other firm was. And even more important than that, you could read the documents strewn around his desk and you had some idea of the work he was doing and perhaps, even identify his clients. You see, we all learned the skill of reading upside down. At least if your eyesight was good enough!

As there was a financial duty imposed on such a transaction, the conveyance was taken to a Stamp Office, the duty paid and a red impression made on the deed. One solicitor with a cruel sense of humour once sent out his articled clerk to go to the

Post Office with the instruction 'Go and buy a 6p [six penny] *impressed* stamp' but with nothing to impress it on!

When I had just opened my practice, I found that some of the established members of the profession were not pleased with the increased competition. Two of them put me through a grueling experience. My client was the purchaser, but I was not then on the panel of solicitors for his building society so when I arranged the completion I had to arrange for the solicitor for the building society (see later) to meet me at the vendor's solicitor's office. Both of them were 'old timers'. To my delight, I was 'double booked', in that I also had a case in the magistrate's court and had to be in court just before the time fixed for the completion. In the rush I did not prepare all the paper work properly and horror upon horrors, I had to hand over £30, which was the only part of the purchase price not covered by the mortgage. Technically, I should have obtained a bank draft for that sum, but in the rush I just took my cheque book. When I offered my cheque, they looked at one another and said words to the effect of "Good heavens, he expects us to deal with his cheque and not a bank draft. It's hardly good enough." In the end the vendor's solicitors took my cheque. Then I was supposed to hand over the free form which was needed to present to the Stamp Office with the Deed. One said to the other 'Good heavens he expects us to supply him with stationery'. I had only been out of the army for a year and had been an officer so I was not used to being treated like that, so I blew my top and told them just what I thought of their arrogant attitude. I assume the word went round that I was not to be played around with, and I never had another similar experience.

In the early 1980s, the government of the day was determined to break the conveyancing monopoly. Austin Mitchell, the M.P. introduced a Private Members Bill which allowed the breach of the monopoly. He was the M.P. for Grimsby but he had been a television journalist and presenter on Yorkshire Television. I was the Law Society spokesman and was asked to enter into a debate with him on the Yorkshire Television current affairs programme, Calendar. I doubt if was ever so apprehensive as I was, as I arrived at the studios. I had never felt as nervous, even when going to court with a difficult case. To my relief, he did not turn up.

In addition to various other types of organisations which I have already mentioned, such as the banks and building societies and Tesco, certain solicitors have created something new altogether. I call them 'conveyancing factories'. A solicitor sets up a separate company or a separate part of his office and advertises a super service. I have noted that this is a service offered by some highly respected firms as well as some smaller firms. I cannot speak as to the quality of their work, although I am told, that all of it is carried out by clerks or former legal secretaries. I am not even sure if they are qualified legal executives. It seems likely that much of this is due to what can be described as commoditised, automated and competitive work. The high street firm has largely been displaced by conveyancing factories. It may be cheaper but the question is, whether or not the service is as good? It cannot possibly be personal in the way that I used to try to provide such a service, but it may be efficient and it may be cheaper.

As a result of Austin Mitchell's bill, the monopoly was broken and a new profession of Licensed Conveyancers was created. Perhaps the general public knows that they are likely to get a better all-round service from a solicitor. Many of those who became Licensed Conveyancers were managing clerks or legal secretaries. It is significant that there were not many of them, so it was not such a threat as we expected. I recollect a former secretary of mine phoning me. It transpired, that she had 'qualified' as a licensed conveyancer but it also transpired that her knowledge was not sufficient, because she was phoning for technical help. I later heard that she had become bankrupt!

There are other ways in which the monopoly can be broken. Early in my career, I helped an estate agent to sort out a problem and from time to time, he would recommend that I act for one of his clients who was selling a house or more often, the purchaser. He was somewhat cynical about solicitors but I reciprocated by matching him with my cynical view of estate agents, contending that we actually worked hard for our money but for the estate agency, at least in those days, was easy-peasy.

His cynicism clearly caused him to look for higher things and he enrolled for a University course and I believe that after graduation he might have attained a master's degree. It was not particularly surprising for me to find that he had 'blown the gaff' on both our professions and had written the equivalent of 'Everyman's guide to property transactions'. I should not advertise such a book but I chanced upon the fact that although he is now long departed, the book 'Bradshaw's House Buying, Selling and Conveyancing', is still in print, now edited by a barrister.

There have been many attempts to simplify the system and speed it up. Now contract and completion frequently take place on the same day. Completions are done by post or email or even on the telephone, with a professional and legally binding undertaking. You don't go to the Stamp Office and you do not use the famous 'IN WITNESS' terminology.

One aspect of the system, is the need to make various searches of a variety of sources. Much information is held by local councils, government registries and other locations. There are standard forms but sometimes the forms require choices to be made. Will one of the discretionary questions be relevant to that property and is my client willing to pay the small extra small fee? Are there other additional questions that should be asked and which should be typed out on the form? This is a particular interest of mine and I have even criticised the Law Society for the weakness of parts of its standard form. I happen to have specialised knowledge of one branch of property law, but it is relatively obscure and I doubt if many solicitors, let alone conveyancers, follow the procedures that I have recommended.[23] However, we are moving towards a completely computerised national system and it will be interesting to see if it is a complete success.

---

23 The article is published in The Conveyancing & Property Lawyer [2013] 77 Conv. Issue 3 186

The pressure and tension of getting the job done is the stuff of nervous breakdowns. There is the so-called 'chain' where each purchaser is dependent upon the completion of a sale and so on, down the line. All must be completed at more or less the same moment, relying on the successful the transfer of funds between the respective banks of the solicitors and also relying on each solicitor, giving a personal and professional undertaking. Similarly, there is probably a small fleet of removal vans waiting for the word 'go' but parked up and down the streets.

The fees now charged are minimal and recent surveys have shown that they are much less than the fees charged by estate agents, which are increasing at a faster rate[24]. There is intense competition. But to be fair, I do not hear as many complaints, except from those who think that it is an expression of their wish to 'kill all the lawyers'.

I would guess that there are many mistakes made because of the lack of expertise and the pressure but I suppose that if the public feels better about it, then although it is helping to kill off the high street solicitor, the public has a won a victory.

I dreamt up, what I thought, was a brilliant marketing gimmick. Because buying a house is usually the biggest transaction in which a person is involved in their lives, I suggested my clients should be given a memento. I wanted to give my clients a plastic imitation quill pen with which they would sign their conveyance or transfer. My partners thought it was a joke and it never happened but I still feel that it would have been a wonderful sales gimmick.

When I first qualified, I learned that if I managed to find someone who would instruct me to act on their behalf when they purchased a house, I would not necessarily be able to act for the building society which was going to lend the money. Building societies had a panel of solicitors and they had to be satisfied that even a qualified solicitor was fully acceptable to them

---

24 LSG 27 April 2015

as someone who should look after their interests. I took issue with at least one building society, arguing that if the Law Society thought that I was good enough to be a solicitor, a building society should respect their judgment and allow me to act for them as a matter of course. Eventually, I found that by arguing with them and also by the fact that I had been placed on one or two panels, I should be entitled to go on the other panels, almost as a right. So I had very little difficulty in convincing them that was a reasonable argument.

And now? We are supposed to be in a free market economy, but there has been a re-introduction of a market restriction by several banks and building societies. They have established approved panels of solicitors and only they can deal with the mortgage documentation. This means, that if the client wishes to have his own solicitor to check and see that the transaction goes through smoothly, he will eventually learn that if that solicitor is not on the approved list of the bank or building society, another firm of solicitors will be appointed by that financial institution to act solely on their behalf. They probably have a standard list of questions, some of which are not relevant to the areas, but they send a list which can be as long as twenty pages and contains as many as sixty questions. These may be reasonable and necessary and the client's own solicitor may have already asked them but there may be just a few where the panel solicitor is being too inquisitive. This leads to more work for the solicitor and also delays. Thus, buyers are being advised that it is in their interests to use a panel solicitor. It is only 'a choice' but in practice, it is pricing the non-panel solicitor out of the market. It could get worse. In Scotland there is already a Separate Representation policy which prevents the same solicitor acting for buyer and the lender. An acquaintance of mine who had his own Scottish specialist conveyancing practice was forced to close down and was fortunate to obtain employment with another firm.

The main lenders such as HSBC, Lloyds Banking Group, Santander and Nationwide all have restricted panels. The solicitor who is denied access to the panel, may appeal but he sometimes has to pay a fee to the lender before he is able to either go on the panel or pursue an appeal. It is no longer a matter of a member of the public being able to choose his own solicitor unless he is prepared to pay that solicitor and also pay the solicitor nominated by the lender to overlook the transaction. It was reported[25] that Metro Bank and Newcastle Building Society now require firms to have at least 120 purchase completions registered with the Land Registry over the previous 12 months.

In addition to knowing the law relating to many aspects of land ownership, sale and purchase, a solicitor must be familiar with the many pages of the Council of Mortgage Lenders Handbook, known colloquially as CML. It covers the requirements of each different lender and the practitioner refers to it frequently. Any breach of the CML is tantamount to an admission of negligence if anything goes wrong and a claim arises.

There is an argument that because the lender is at risk and if there is anything wrong with the title, the lender may not recover all that he has lent. However, solicitors are covered by indemnity insurance and it seems to me that this practice is unfair to a member of the public who has great faith in his own particular solicitor, who he has probably known for some time.

There are problems such as property fraud. There was a major change in property law in 1925 and most of us would be able to quote sections of the Law of Property Act of that year or one of the associated statutes. At the same time, the concept of registration of title was introduced, but it took 50 years before it is really took over the property market. Instead of those lovely deeds that I have already described, you simply have registration of title at the Land Registry. At first, you used to have a Land Certificate which guaranteed the title but now property registration is based on computer records, rather than paper title deeds. There has always been fraud, but the new method of 'proving' title is so much easier. A chap claims to have lost his deeds and applies to

---

25 LSG 5 October 2015

the Land Registry for a duplicate set and to all intents and purposes he can sell someone else's house.

Another problem is that of the bogus firm of solicitors. They claim to be a legitimate firm and appear to have the right sort of notepaper and follow all the proper procedures but they are just fraudsters who, when the purchase money is paid over to them, just pocket it and disappear. The Solicitors Regulation Authority reported that the number of reports about bogus firms is rising. In 2013 the SRA dealt with 548 reports of people purporting to be legitimate firms of solicitors, an increase of 57 on 2012 and it was going up. The Authority places the responsibility on the solicitor dealing with them to check to ensure that they are legitimate.[26]

One practitioner was quoted in the newspaper as explaining that it is part of the overall increase in chronic fraud rather than particular to the electronic register. Apparently there are cases where someone is able to obtain access to the Land Registry and to arrange the sale of property especially if it is not occupied. Apparently property fraud has cost the Land Registry £2.5 million one year and £1.5 million in another year because it guarantees the title and has to pay the loss out of its indemnity fund. You need professional discipline to act responsibly to avoid this type of fraud, although I must concede that there are a few – just a few – solicitors who fail to live up to the standards which are required.

The Solicitors Regulation authority has said[27]:

> 'More and more reports are being received of firms either being contacted by con artists or falling victim to fraudulent activity, with potentially serious consequences for clients buying or selling property. The SRA is urging solicitors to step up their efforts to keep criminals out and protect client interests.

---

26 LSG 10 November 2014
27 Press Statement 1 June 2015

The majority of recent scams fall into two categories:
- Firms receiving calls pretending to be banks to obtain sensitive information, such as account passwords
- Emails between firms and clients being intercepted, leading to client funds being paid into fraudsters' accounts

This is against a backdrop of continued instances of con artists pretending to be solicitors, using either fake names or stealing the identities of genuine firms'

The Times explained[28] that Russian gangs were targeting solicitors in a fraud that allowed them to steal cash on the day of completion. It was seen as a 'Friday afternoon fraud' which in six weeks had cost the profession (they called it an industry) £50 million.

> 'Typically solicitors are conned into changing the account into which they pay the money for the house purchase. The plots involve a combination of identity fraud and cyber techniques, such as hacking, malware and spear phishing – sending an email that appears to be from a bank or organisation known or recognisable to the target.'

I may have concerns as to how IT could make conveyancing so impersonal and unable to cope with the uncertainties and the unexpected situation, but I await seeing if a recent innovation is a real solution to some problems. The Law Society is about to launch its conveyancing portal. It will bring together, electronically, all the processes, checks and documentation prepared and undertaken by solicitors and licensed conveyancers in the sale and purchase of residential properties. The fee will be £20 and will include money laundering searches and conveyancing forms. As the Land Registry says that there were 1,974,000 residential property transactions in the UK in 2013, one can hope for a major streamlining of the procedures which will enable most of

---

28 4 September 2015

the communications between a conveyancing professional and home movers to take place online, cutting postal costs. I wait with baited breath.[29]

So is conveyancing professional work? I suggest that if it is properly done, then it is the work of a professional, but the conveyancing factories cannot claim to be professional. It is a trade. The introduction of the registered land system encourages simple repetitive property transfers but I wonder how often things go wrong. They definitely form part of the 190% increase in claims for negligent practice which I report later.

As one person put it – experience is gradually being replaced by clever computer systems which generate a set procedure for each transaction.

Of course there is now the new *purported* profession of Licensed Conveyancer. It seems to be a contradiction, that there are two real professions who do the same things, so overall, I no longer consider it to be the work of a profession.

Is it good for Joe Public?

I have several ways of answering this question. One is to say that the jury is still out. The other is to remind myself of the man who was looking for the one handed lawyer. I consider that there have been some substantial benefits for the public. Conveyancing is competitive and therefore, there is a chance that a member of the public can save money. On the other hand he no longer has the choice of his own solicitor, because of the restrictions now imposed by banks and building societies.

I know that many people have criticised the concept that there should be an exchange of contracts and then a time gap before the actual completion. In Scotland it does not work like that. Nowadays, even in England, you get the contract and completion on the same day. I still do not know if this is in the interest of the public. It is all too rushed and for a short time, uncertain. However, the other side of the coin, is that you do not have the same

---

29 LSG 9 March 2015

standard of checking of title. It is not just a matter of ownership, but also of understanding whether or not the property is correctly described and whether it has the right easements, namely rights of way and light and drainage and so on. To get it right, is a great skill and I have a constant worry that factory conveyancers, dealing with these transactions, do not know sufficient enough about the surrounding law, to be able to get it right. But put together, the fall in cost and the speeding up of the transaction I feel that on balance, it is good for Joe Public.

Is it good for the common attorney? No – it definitely is not, especially so far as his pocket and his nerves are concerned. One has to admit that 'in the old days' conveyancing was a leisurely activity. Mostly, this was because of some legal issues but admittedly, partly due to the failings of the profession. But I still believe that conveyancing had been the bread-and-butter work of a solicitor and sometimes, the fact that he was earning relatively easy money from that activity, meant that he could subsidise some of the other work that he did, making being a practicing solicitor reasonably profitable. The competition, the streamlining and the power of the estate agents, building societies and banks have made this a nightmare for the common attorney. It is bad but there are worse issues as we will see.

CHAPTER 4

WILLS AND PROBATE

It was traditional for a solicitor to charge a nominal fee for drafting most wills. It was looked upon as a loss leader because you usually kept the signed will in your safe and when the client died you would almost certainly be instructed to prove the will (obtain Probate) and administer the estate. The latter was where the profit lay. It was said that the value of a solicitors' practice could be established by counting the number of wills that he had in the safe.

The law relating to wills has hardly changed for decades. The will must be signed by the maker (the testator) in front of two witnesses who must sign to say that they witnessed the signing. The will remains in existence as a legal document even if the maker changed his mind. The only ways in which it could be shown that he had changed his mind are if he formally revoked it in writing, or if by the action of burning, tearing or otherwise destroying it, he robustly showed that such was his intention.

A chap made his will in favour of what is now known as his live in boyfriend and excluded all the members of his family. When this became known to the family, after his death, they were upset and the boyfriend was upset, so everyone was upset. The boyfriend was so distraught that he went into the solicitors who held the will and collected it. He wandered the streets and then put it in a waste paper basket. An hour or so later, he changed his mind and went back to search for it, but it had gone. He asked us to obtain probate and because he could prove the existence of the will after death and because the previous solicitors could give evidence of the contents, we were able to help him to obtain Probate. Obviously emotion plays a large part in this and I was pleased when our new client decided to give part of the estate to his lover's family.

Wills can be matters of family dispute. We all had at least one client who came to change her will every few months, as she fell out with one or other of her sisters or brothers, her nieces or her nephews or her friends. It was unfair on the one with whom she last fell out!

I was often asked to advise, as to what a client should do with his or her estate, but I always explained that it was not my function. If a client asked for advice about bequests to charities, I used to hand them one of the guides to charities published by the legal press and say 'You choose'.

A particularly difficult situation is where someone becomes an old person's 'best friend' and takes advantage of the situation by exercising 'undue influence'. I drew a couple of wills for a lady who explained that she was excluding some of her nephews because they were the children of the richest of her sisters. When she died I learned that although I had been her adviser for many years, she had made a new will in hospital shortly before her death and I learned that the excluded nephews were included and some of the others excluded. I learned that their mother had visited my client's house after she was admitted to hospital and found a copy of the will, which I had drafted. She then brought another solicitor to the hospital and had a new will prepared and signed. The new version now included the formerly excluded grandsons, but excluded some of the originally named beneficiaries. Although I was certain that there had been undue influence it was not medically provable because although it had been witnessed by two nurses each of them said that they could not remember any of the surrounding circumstances.

It had been the privilege of the legal profession to draft wills. However, as stationers sell homemade will forms or you can download one from the internet, members of the public can write their wishes using such forms and intending it to be their will. Frequently, they do not do so with sufficient clarity or certainty or do not follow the rules about the witnesses to the signature and the resulting arguments are a profitable consequence for lawyers.

Then the monopoly of drafting wills was lost and we now see will making services offered by banks and building societies. There is also an Institute of Professional Will Makers. I doubt if they really offer a loss leader of a cheap will and it is also out of fashion for solicitors to do so. Whether they give the same service will become apparent as the testator becomes the deceased!

Associated with the making of wills is the 'proving' of wills, the procedure of obtaining probate. This has attracted almost as much opprobrium as even conveyancing. There are some people, who before death, are able to put their affairs in order so that it is easy for the executor but few people with a range of assets such as stocks and shares, bank and building society accounts and insurance policies actually leave their affairs in apple pie order.

The person entrusted by him to call[30] in the estate and then carry out the wishes of the deceased and the payment of any Inheritance tax– the executor – who then does it all himself or, if the assets of the estate of the testators intentions are complicated, he employs either a bank or, hopefully, a solicitor. In theory the work of 'calling in the' the estate should be completed in a year – 'the executor's year' – after which the executor becomes a trustee to administer the estate.

Sometimes, just establishing what the deceased actually owned and its value can require a whole series of letters to banks, insurance companies and other assets in which the testator had invested, so it can be a long winded process. Arguments with the Revenue and even complying with the requirements of the Probate Registry needs the patience of a solicitor and a great deal of persistence. This has led to regular criticism on two counts. The first is that many solicitors are very slow and the other is that the costs are excessive.

---

30 'Calling in' is the process of gathering together all the assets and selling them or otherwise turning them into cash or sorting out the title to assets preparatory to distributing them as planned by the testator.

I have a suspicion that the problems and complaints about the speed of completing the administration have an element of truth. I feel that if a solicitor has ten matters to deal with, on a particular day, the matters which involve live clients who are often on the phone or calling in to find out what progress there is, will be his first priority. There is no live client to cause that activity. There may be the beneficiaries who would like to get their hands on the money, but they are probably not the people who are the regular clients of the solicitor. In many cases, they are not part of the goodwill of the practice. The criticism which this attracts is well known and dragging down the image of the profession.

Costs were a major issue. Once, it was a matter of holding the file, weighing it and deciding how much it was worth. For many years, factors such as the value of the estate and the difficulty were elements taken into consideration when fixing the fee. Now, the solicitor must prove how much time was involved, whether the time was spent properly and apply his charging rate, as I described earlier.

Many people take the opportunity of giving money or property to a charity in their will and the major charities are adept at keeping track of the progress of the administration of estates, where they are to receive some benefit. They monitor the grants of probate and if they do not hear from the solicitor, or other executor speedily and regularly, they keep up a dialogue to make sure that there is progress.

At one time, I was a member of a panel set up by the Law Society, to check whether the charges claimed by a solicitor were fair and reasonable. An unfortunately high proportion were about the administration of estates. In most cases, I found that if the solicitor was efficient, then the matter progressed at a reasonable pace his charges would be justified. Sometimes, although the complaint was about costs, I noticed that the beneficiary was still unhappy, because of the tardiness of the solicitor. The solicitor could not win. I thought that those complaining might have been told, that you don't buy a Mini and expect a Rolls Royce at the same price.

The only real threat to the solicitor's virtual monopoly was the banking industry. They were allowed to offer probate and administration services, but I suspect that many members of the public distrust the banks even more than they distrust lawyers. In particular and correctly, they know or believe that even if solicitors are expensive, it is likely that the banks will be even more expensive. But now there are even greater threats.

There are now licensed will drafting firms, which are only lightly regulated and one writer in the Law Society Gazette[31] tells horrific stories of their positively harmful practices. In the same issue of the Gazette, it is reported that the Institute of Chartered Accountants was applying to become a probate regulator, thus allowing 140,000 chartered accountants to offer probate services by the end of 2013.

About 180,000 wills were written in 2013 by non-lawyers but I am not aware of how many were drafted by the 2000 members of the Society of Will Writers.[32] The Legal Ombudsman would like to see clients having access for redress for poor services by Will Writers but for some strange and unexplained reason, they are not regulated, although the members of the Society would welcome a volunteer scheme.

Drafting a will is not just about the words that you use. Many follow a fairly standard form, but at the present time, it is much more about advice on mitigating Inheritance Tax and also about understanding the dynamics of the client's family.

Is it still the work of a professional? Once again, I consider that it is a contradiction that several different disciplines offer to draw wills and obtain probate and administer an estate. So, it is no longer the work of a professional. It may be the work of a person with skills, but a person who needs such a service no longer looks to one group professing a particular skill.

So is it good for the common attorney? Obviously not. He has lost a lucrative part of his work but it is his own fault. He

---

31 Marie Granby 15 July 2013
32 LSG 20 October 2014

was slow, expensive and surrounded the whole process with mystique.

Is it good for Joe Public? On balance I have to say 'yes'. He has seen that he can do it himself or that he can go to someone who he fears. He fears the latter because we have attracted opprobrium and much of it related to this branch of legal practice. Perhaps Joe will not gain all the benefits that he seeks. My family had some dealings with a person offering the alternative service and a simple job ended up with a solicitor being called in, to sort out the mess. I hope that this was just an exception.

CHAPTER 5

LICENSING

I don't really know how I entered the field of licensing law. It was a branch of the legal practice which had a fairly bad reputation, from the point of view of a practising solicitor. The slightest mistake in procedure meant that you had to start again from the beginning and the magistrates who formed the licensing committee of the bench had a fearsome reputation, in most towns including mine. They were sticklers for detail and very restrictive about the grant of new licences. And they were right. As alcohol has become part of the British culture, so have the stringent requirements of licensing law, been relaxed. One feeds upon the other and now, almost anyone can get a licence anywhere and it is likely to become easier. There are more and more pubs and clubs and more and more drunkenness. I am a drinker but some may say that I am a killjoy, because I argue that drink leads to violence and general abandonment of good moral standards. There can be little doubt that the club culture and drink and drugs go hand in hand. Sometimes, when I pass through town in the late evening and I see the girls in the most skimpy of dresses (dresses – is that what they are?). I understand why there are some people, including judges, who think that they are offering an invitation for sex. I will not include myself, because I will be accused of being sexist. Heaven forbid!

I can claim that my involvement with licensing was largely different.

When I started my practice, there were many off licences, particularly corner shops, which sold some 'booze'. At one time, it was also common for a chemist's shop to have a licence. Perhaps it was then thought that 'drink' was actually good for health!

At first, my main licensing work was to oppose applications for new *off* licences, but later I also started to deal with pubs and clubs with *on* licences.[33]

After having carried out a couple of off license applications, in which I succeeded, despite objections from nearby off licensees, I got a call from the Off License Holders Association. To this day, I don't know why they instructed me as, in truth, I knew no more about licensing than the next man. Although these cases were heard in the magistrates' court, which is essentially, but not exclusively, a criminal court, there is one major difference compared with most magistrates' jurisdictions. They were dealt with by a committee of justices who could develop and apply a local policy. In those days, the policy was a secret matter, which the magistrates applied but did not disclose and therefore one had to interpret the decisions of the committee, over a period of time to learn what their undeclared policy was. There were some principles, which they announced from time to time and their annual report gave some clues. I think that I must have managed to understand their policy by intuition, more than by knowledge.

A known factor was that they did not want too many outlets for the sale of alcohol. The number of off license shops in any one area and the density of population were important factors. Another known feature was that off licences were free from some of the more stringent provisions of the Shops Act about closing hours, so that they could remain open late in the evenings.

'Need' was the buzz word. So I used to tease out the reasons for anyone applying and often got them to admit that contrary to their claims, that it was a busy shop and that their customers *needed* them to have a licence, the truth was that business was not very good and they really needed to do anything possible to

---

33 As the names imply an off licence was to sell alcohol for consumption off i.e. away from the premises whereas an on licence allowed the customer to consume the alcohol on or in the premises as well as to buy it to take it home.

increase takings and profitability, by staying open later and later. Another factor was that bottled goods have a longer shelf life and thus if a shopkeeper invests in bottled stock, it does not go off as quickly as fruit and vegetables. As 'sell by dates' became the norm, it was also apparent that many other goods were more or less time limited. Many of the shops were small corner shops with limited space, limited stock and turnover.

When I was in court to oppose applications, I developed techniques of cross-examination and tactics which were very successful. The main one, was to ask about the variety of stock and ask what their customers wanted to buy. I would have carried out a site visit in advance and sometimes, I counted the number of different types of biscuit, or sometimes the varieties of tea or coffee or cereals. I would ask them to accept that a reasonable shop would stock, say two or three times as many varieties of biscuits, tea coffee or cereals, than they did. I suggested that they were not interested in their customers' needs but their own aspirations. They found it hard to disagree with me. But the best was that I would go on to ask if their customers ate fruit and vegetables and when they agreed, I was almost always able to get them to admit that they had very little or no such goods in the shop. I would then ask 'isn't it better to use the available space for healthy fruit and vegetables instead of *booze*?'

Quite often, the crunch question was "Why don't you use the space to stock fresh fish?" And the magistrates told me informally, that they enjoyed great amusement, as they waited for the 'fresh fish' question to be asked and assess the answer. But one applicant gave me my comeuppance. His reply was 'Why stock fresh fish when the van from Whitby comes twice a week.'

Most of my cases were in Leeds, but some other committees in the region, were very similar. But Bradford changed its approach to licensing, from time to time. I remember going through my routine on one occasion and heard one magistrate whisper to another, in a carrying tone, "Why is he wasting our time with this sort of question?" I lost!

Since 1971, solicitors had a right of audience in the Crown Courts. I exercised my rights on a few occasions, especially in licensing appeals, but actually never felt absolutely comfortable. In one particular case, I was up against the late Gerald Lumley, then one of the best barristers on the North Eastern circuit and as is probably par for the course, he tried every technique of persuasion even *before* the case started. The good point was that my wife who had hardly ever heard me in court, came in to hear part of the case and has regularly reminded me that she ended up by being sorry for the witnesses that I cross examined. Fortunately, I won the appeal.

There was another and funny point about that case. When I checked the shop, I found that the owner had not one, but two or three 'top shelves'. In other words, he had several shelves of soft porn magazines which were not quite high enough to make it difficult for small children to get hold of them. As the shop was near a school, I made great play of this and coined the phrase that he was wanting to run a 'porn and port shop'!

Whilst referring to 'porn' I am reminded of a later development in my licensing practice. I sometimes did apply for, or oppose, a licence for pubs and clubs and sometimes, even acted for the police in opposing applications or renewals of licences. There was a group of demolition men in the Leeds and Bradford area, several of whom, I had represented in a number of matters from company acquisitions, conveyancing, crime and civil disputes. I knew that AB was no longer instructing me. I also knew, because it was reported in detail in the local press, that he was running a drinking club of sorts just outside Leeds. He was also flagrantly ignoring planning law and the planners were trying to control his operations.

He was also running terribly pornographic shows with audience participation. A photographer from a local paper attended with a miniature camera strapped to his leg and took photographs of the 'lewd performances'. This came into the possession of the police who duly prosecuted him to conviction. When his licence came up for renewal they decided to object and instructed me to appear for them. I asked AB about the shows and he denied that there was anything wrong at least with anything under his control. I therefore started to put the photographs to him one by one. I am sure the magistrates were enjoying it but AB was not. When the pressure was on him, he responded to one question by saying "Jerry, why are you being so hard on me?" Everyone in the court collapsed in laughter! The licence was revoked.

I also acted for the Leeds and District Licensed Victuallers Association, in other words the trade protection organisation for local publicans. Whilst I found the off-licence holders would oppose an application and if granted, would immediately ask the new licencee to join the organisation and offer them help, the publicans were most upset if a licence was granted in the face of their opposition. Their cases were always what I would describe as 'heavy'.

But the publicans are delightful people to know. However, they managed to con me on one occasion in no uncertain manner. Three of four of them had been in to see me about a routine matter and just as they were leaving, the President paused by the door and said:

"Jerry, would you like to be the chairman at our annual banquet?"

I felt really honoured and said "Yes". There was a short pause and he said

"You know that you have to pay for the top table drinks?"
'That's OK" I said.
"Oh, and the pre-dinner reception?"

I hesitated a little but I could say nothing but "OK, then" I think they got through the door and then came back a little.

"There is the printing of the menu."
"Yes" I said guardedly.

"And the tickets."

I was in so deep there was no way out.

"Did you mention the main raffle prize?' said one.
"No. What sort of prize?"
"A portable TV would be just right." (They were quite expensive in those days)

I couldn't say anything. They went into reception and then the President came back:

"It's the toastmaster. You pay for him, of course, but he won't drive home at night anymore so there will be overnight accommodation for him; and his wife comes with him, you know. Anyway, you will need him because he introduces you before you make your speech."

By then I was too punch drunk to speak.

And so it was an extremely expensive event for my firm. It was one of my activities that did not make my partners very happy, especially as they were not invited to the banquet.

There was a sequel.

The next year they reverted to normal and had a representative from one of the breweries as chairman. They told me the date and I put it in my diary. For the dinner I had had to wear a chain of office which I was to keep for the year. They reminded me that I would have to return it at the next year's dinner. One night, a week, before the diary date, I had a phone call at home. "Where are you and where is the chain?" said a familiar voice. Apparently, they had changed the date and forgotten to tell me. They had not sent me a ticket and it was too late to go. Red faces all round.

On a more serious note, some of the pubs in one part of Leeds, started to have a great problem with 'travellers'. These were caravan dwellers who moved around the country and set up camps, wherever they found some vacant land. They had found such a site in South Leeds, near a group of pubs. They were heavy drinkers, but could not take their drink. They were constantly fighting and causing damage and scaring away the regular customers. The publicans started to exclude them. In the trade it is known as 'clotching'.[34] This resulted in a complaint to the Commission for Racial Equality. The travellers claimed they were either gypsies or came within the definition of a gypsy in law. I carried out a great deal of research into the law relating to Racial Discrimination and also Caravan Sites. In addition, I read extensively, about gypsies and their origin which is a most fascinating subject. I suggested that the publicans erected signs saying:

"No travellers other than ethnic gypsies allowed."

I also suggested that we inform the Commission of our proposal and ask them to confirm that it was legal. The Commission called us to a meeting, but in the morning I received a phone call from someone claiming to act on behalf of the Gypsy Council. He told me that a Jew should not act against gypsies. That, as Hitler had tried to wipe out the gypsies as well as the Jews, I was helping my own enemies. He hinted that if the gypsies were excluded then I had better watch my back. I reported this to the Commission officials but they never told me of the result of my complaint. They did however refuse to condone the notice. As the law stood then, they were probably correct because there was at least one case about caravan legislation, which did equate travellers with gypsies. It was eventually repealed, but I

---

34 'Clotching' seems to be a particularly Leeds word. It meant excluding a customer from the pub either permanently or for a period of time. I read about a local mayor being so excluded and I wrote to 'The Times' telling readers that in Leeds it was called 'clotching'. I thought that other readers would claim that it was in use elsewhere but no one made such a claim or make any comment about such an unusual word.

have noticed very recently that a court has made another very similar ruling in another case.

Licensing law, policy and practice has gone through many changes, especially since the Licensing Act 2003 and it is no longer an interesting activity. Soon after the Act became law, I went into a courtroom, thinking that it was the licensing court and the clerk said jokingly "Licensing. Hasn't it been abolished?"

There is a long history of the law being used to control the supply of alcohol. Sometimes it has been to ensure that, if the government wished to obtain some easy money from the public. alcohol was an easy target because it was the drug of the masses. The fact that they needed their drink meant that the government had an easy way of applying a tax or duty on the production or sale of drink. Sometimes control was applied because of drunkenness. There is a fascinating examination of liquor licensing in the 'History of Liquor Licensing in England and Wales.'[35] It is described as 'experiments in licensing policy' as the level of control waxed and waned. The gin palaces of the eighteenth century were a source of excessive drunkenness and were therefore controlled by restricting the number of outlets, but sometimes for purely political purposes. But there was what they called 'legislative repentance'. This was fuelled by the emergence of the Temperance Societies. During the First World War control was made stricter, so as to stop the workers in munitions factories getting inebriated at lunchtime.

The reasons for the loss of public houses are diverse, from the effect of the breathalyser, the restriction on smoking inside the pub to competition from cheap supermarket beer. Whatever the reasons, it is a sad sight to see so many former pubs closed and derelict or being converted into houses and shops.

At least, I had years of fun. In my work, I read widely and I chanced upon the following:

---

35 Sydney and Beatrice Webb. English Local Government Series

The Vintners Company, one of the London guilds had for many, many years a certain exemption. It was known in the reign of King George II and seems to have existed well before that. The exemption was recorded in Section 199 (1) Licensing Act 1964 as 'exemption from the requirement to take out a justices' licence enjoyed by the Company of the master, warden and commonality of Vintners of the City of London'.

Patterson's Licensing Law [106th edition] explained

'Although they had to observe licensing hours, there was a charter of 2nd February 1611 for the benefit of the freemen of the company and 'also for the better maintenance of our subjects being sailors of our kingdom of England' which enabled the freemen to sell wine in the City of London and 'also in all other cities and towns know by the name of 'thoroughfare towns' where our courtiers commonly called posts, were set up and limited to, in the common road usually frequented and used by foreigners or natives ... between London and Berwick, wheresoever any freeman or freemen of the mistery aforesaid now dwell or dwelleth or hereafter shall happen to dwell'.

On 7th June 1889 the Vintners' Company issued to their members an order defining the area over which the privilege could be exercised and the 'thoroughfare towns' included cities and towns on the post roads, one of which was described as the road between London and Berwick

The post towns included Waltham, South Witham (Lincolnshire), Grantham, Newark, Tuxford, Scrooby, Doncaster, Ferrybridge, Tadcaster, York Wetherby, Boroughbridge, Catterick, Bowes, Burghe, Penrith, Carlisle, Northallerton, Darlington, Durham, Newcastle-upon-Tyne, Hexham, Thirwall, Morpeth, Alnwick, Belford, and Berwick on the road from London to Berwick.'

Whilst this list is clearly wider than the Great North Road, the Great North Road was clearly one of two special roads to which the Vintners were referring.

The exemption was revoked by Section 196 Licensing Act 2003.

I actually wrote to the Vintners' Society many years ago enquiring about membership, but was 'diplomatically' discouraged from pursuing my enquiry!!! Clearly, my name or face did not fit or I was an upstart. Strangely, many years later, because I became a member of another n City Guild, several of our dinners are held in the Vintners' Hall. So I got there after all!

I rather liked another historical comment. When there was a proposal for a stamp duty on articles of clerkship in the early nineteenth century a lawyer complained 'that LAW like Beer is now sold by RETAIL by HIS MAJESTY'S ROYAL ANNUAL FEE'.[36]

Is it work for professionals? I suggest that because of the importance in the social fabric, it should be. I do not know if there are still any contested licensing applications, other than when the police try to have a licensed premise closed down. This was such a specialised field that there were few common attorneys who dared enter the fray. Therefore, the changes in the law are of no particular consequence to the common attorney. I can only assume that as this is work that requires several skills, it will remain the work of a professional.

The changes are not good for Joe Public. This is not a matter of legal practice. It is a matter of public policy.

What concerns me, is that there is so much more drinking that it is now a social disaster. There is so much more uncontrolled activity or even violence. I think that this has been a disaster for Joe Public. Whilst it was strictly controlled, licensing of alcoholic refreshment was good for the public. It no longer is. Decisions about liquor licensing are now made by

---

36 Quoted by Roberts (Op Cit) P17

a committee of the local council and not by the magistrates. The magistrates had also dealt with problems which arise from excessive drinking and they knew the gravity of the problem. Local councilors will never have had that specialised knowledge or experience.

Is it good for the common attorney? Unfortunately not. It was a branch of legal practice that required the skills of an advocate, but was not too complicated for a reasonably skilled solicitor. Nevertheless he has lost most of the work. Is does seem that only a few specialist firms who act, for instance, for breweries or night club owners, are still required rendering it a great loss.

CHAPTER 6

DIVORCE AND OTHER MARITAL MATTERS

Cary Grant allegedly said that divorce was a game played by lawyers!

There have probably been greater changes in this branch of the law than any other and probably none of which, have contributed to the sidelining of solicitors than the law and practice dealing with what once were described as 'matrimonial affairs' The changes are mainly relating to the restriction on public funding. This branch of law was practiced in the part of the High Court known as the 'Probate, Divorce and Admiralty Division' and it should not be a surprise that the most frequent typo was by a secretary who typed Probate, Divorce and *Adultery* Division'. I suppose that it was a Freudian slip. Now it is the Family Division. Sometimes journalists describe this branch of the law, simply, as 'Family'.

There was a time when someone who wanted to end a marriage had to prove that his or her spouse had committed a matrimonial offence, such as having been cruel, committed adultery or deserted the other. Even then, the grant of a decree of divorce was in the discretion of the judge who had to decide whether or not one of these matrimonial offences had been committed and the burden of proof was what is described as 'on the balance of probabilities'. In adultery cases, it was known that sometimes, a sham situation was created, such as a spouse booking a hotel room and being joined by a stooge companion. Somewhat by coincidence, an enquiry agent would knock on the door and see the couple embracing, or perhaps, he just noticed that the bedclothes were crumpled and that was, hopefully, enough proof of adultery. If the petitioner had himself committed adultery he had to put in a 'Discretion Statement' in a sealed envelope telling of all his exploits. It was always said that there was at least one local judge who found his name listed as one who had given rise to the application for discretion and, indeed I had a Bradford client who insisted on the case being heard in Leeds because she assured me that one of the local judges would appear in her list. There was also a gentleman known as the Queen's Proctor who was on the lookout for people who misled the court. He checked to see if the husband had simply spent a night in a hotel with a paid friend and he would ask the chambermaid if the bed had actually been disturbed.

I was establishing a reasonable matrimonial practice even before I married, although I used to argue that in order to be a fully equipped solicitor you really should be able to drive a car, have bought a house of your own, been married and had children. Just before I married and by happenchance I took a book off the shelves of the local public library called 'Lawyer heal thyself'. It was the story of a solicitor who specialised in matrimonial cases. He became so wrapped up in his client's marital problems that he did not think about his own marriage and it started to fall down around him. But it was too late and his own divorce soon followed. After I read it, I urged my then fiancée to read it and after she did so, she showed it to one of her uncles who was also a solicitor. He advised her not to marry a solicitor! Fortunately, she ignored his advice. A few years later, I often found myself reading a file for a contested matrimonial case or looking at the relevant law last thing at night and sometimes, after we had both gone to bed. Sometimes I would urge her to read part of the file and then say to her "Aren't you glad that you are not married to someone like that?"

We have a friend married to a former barrister. She told of a case in which her husband had acted and one of the allegations of cruelty was a particular sexual activity. She expressed amusement because it was their favourite method. It takes all sorts to make a world!

There was also a way in which an aggrieved party who did not want a divorce, or because the procedure was swifter but who wanted to obtain maintenance and so on, could do so by applying for a separation order in the magistrates court. The grounds for an order from the magistrates included an additional ground which was 'wilful neglect to maintain'. It was a route which was available to those who did not believe in divorce, possibly for religious reasons.

I well recollect a lady who asked for such an order. She told me of her husband's conduct. His sexual demands were excessive – too frequent and at the wrong times. She was upset because they lived in one of those back to back houses, so common in Leeds and the noise of their frequent activity would be heard by the neighbours. I assured her that what she described was cruel and that she could obtain her order on those grounds. "No," she said "it's that he can't maintain me because he is so tired from his activities, that he can't get up to go to work so we're short of money." She contacted me before the hearing to say that they had become reconciled – he had promised to go to work more often.

There were grounds for ending a marriage by annulment. The grounds were non – consummation or wilful refusal to consummate a marriage. I had a case when my client, the woman, was respondent and her husband was saying that it was she who refused to consummate. She was upset by that, because she told me that he was just covering up his inadequacy. She claimed that it was his inability that was the cause. The judge heard the two parties and listened to the cross examination. My barrister turned to me when he had almost finished his cross examination and enquired if there were any other questions that I thought that he should ask. I suggested that if it was the wife who was at fault, how was the husband so certain that he was ready, willing and able (or words to that effect). The question was asked and he answered "I know because the voices tell me". That was the end of his case.

I was amazed, when about seventy years after the event, we stumbled upon the records which showed that we had a very unusual occurrence in my family. My grandfather's second marriage turned out to be very unsuccessful and his second wife applied to the court for restitution of conjugal rights, a remedy which no longer exists.[37] The parties resolved their differences before the court had to order restitution.

I once made a terrible mistake. I was a spokesman for the legal profession in my area and was once taking part in a radio phone in. A woman came on the line and asked "Me 'usband's left us and I want the 'ouse in my name." I responded "Well it's not as easy as that. You have to start divorce proceedings and ask for a transfer of property order." She interrupted and said "It's not a divorce I want. Me 'usband's died!"

I know that many felt that Leo Abse's Divorce Law Reform Act was a breakthrough in easing the lives of many who were in unhappy marriages from which they could not escape but, I felt and still feel that it was a leap too far.

Now divorce is by consent or by proving as little as two years' separation. The breakdown need not be due to a matrimonial offence. We were told that we had to discuss the possibility of reconciliation and sign a certificate to that effect. Within months of the introduction of the new law, I found young people coming into the office for a divorce. They did not ask for it, they demanded it. They did not want to talk about reconciliation and would not try to heal a damaged relationship. Now there are just two issues to argue about and with which the lawyer has to help. One is the children – 'the interest of the child is paramount'. The other is money.

In my early days, even undefended divorces were the exclusive province of barristers but soon we were allowed to present such cases to the judge. We were fortunate in my town because we had a wonderful County Court Judge, 'Dom' McKee. He was the archetypal wise old judge, kind and helpful as long as you were trying to do things in the right way. He would ask you in for a chat after his last case of the day and he was a benevolent influence upon we young lawyers. If you were getting it wrong he would help and if you helped he would show appreciation. I

---

37 An order that the relevant spouse returns home and resumes married life.

am sure that by acting in that way he gave us all confidence and helped set a good standard.

There was however a day when I sent an assistant solicitor to appear on one such undefended case. He was wearing a bright yellow shirt which was then the fashion, but of course round his neck he had his stiff white winged collar and tabs. After pronouncing the decree nisi, the Judge said to my assistant "Which football team do you play for?" He never again wore a coloured shirt in court!

Now, if you are going to be a successful matrimonial lawyer you have to be able to help screw the most money out of the other spouse. Lawyers claim to be able to help people though divorce but what they can do sometimes is to raise the temperature. One solicitor who tells the world through the media that helpful mediation is the way to sort out a failed marriage is so aggressive that she is known as the 'barracuda'. The best of these lawyers is the one who understands money and has the ability to explore a financial position even though there is not really enough for two former spouses and the children. But we were still left with the interests of the children. The courts brought in the social workers and it became a matter of psychology and guessing who could do least harm to the children.

The newspapers no longer attract the prurient interest about stories of sex and cruelty, so they revel in the details of the finances and the attempts by some who have earned the family fund, to keep a part, possibly too much of it. The classic divorce lawyers are those who represent the Heather Mills and Paul McCartneys and the Princess Diana and Prince of Wales of this world.

It seemed as though it could not get worse, but then the government decided there could no longer be legal aid to help solve the problems which affect the children. So warring parents with limited means no longer have the services of skilled professionals. Helpful caring sympathetic solicitors are no more.

The government wants to funnel money into the National Health Service. Medicine costs more and more because medical science becomes more and more complex and expensive. Medicine might cure the wounded and sick, but the psychological scars caused by warring parents will not have the benefit of legal medicine or legal doctors.

Once, it was not possible to have a pre-nuptial agreement (a 'pre-nup') because it was only the court which could decide how much one spouse could gain from the other, but the law is gradually – I would suggest inexorably – moving towards pre-nups. So what is the attorney to tell his client and what to do on his behalf? His duty is to gain the best for his client. Some lawyers, whilst acting like piranhas, claim that they are making future life better for their client but I have known cases where the parties have themselves, decided on an amicable split of the assets and a reasonable amount of financial support, but the lawyer has intervened. No doubt he suggests that what was agreed is insufficient or 'the court will not approve it' and so the merry-go-round starts until one or other falls off.

But what is certain, is that a financially poor spouse, has been suffering and will suffer much more in the future. There were many solicitors who chose to practise matrimonial law who did so with a large helping of sympathy and good intentions. One who would hold the hand of a nervous man or woman, who is desperately unhappy, confused and uncertain. A lawyer who has a big box of tissues in the drawer to mop up the tears. One who goes to the court house with his client and gives words of encouragement. One who knows the procedures and who can guide his client through the ordeal of giving evidence and who can commiserate if despite his efforts things go wrong. He will no longer be available, at least not if he expects to be paid for his services, not even the pittance that he has recently been paid. He made sure that his client had access to justice.

In the Law Society Gazette it was recorded[38] that one firm had created a 'digital tool' of a divorce app, rated by the Sunday Times as one of the world's 'top 500 apps'. It is free to download

---

38 Law Society Gazette 29 November 2012

to iPhone and iPad. Lawyers explain the answers to frequently asked questions on divorce, finance and family law. Charts map the legal procedures which clients will encounter and the timing of financial settlements. Common legal terms are explained. I just cannot imagine many of my clients having the ability or staying power to comply with all the necessary steps. Their emotional state is such that they often cannot act in a controlled manner.

Public Funding (it used to be called 'Legal Aid') has been withdrawn for family matters.

According to the web site of DivorceAid, changes to legal aid mean that pre- 1st April 2013, people on low incomes were eligible for legal aid to cover all aspects of family disputes, including divorce, children (such as contact and residence disputes), financial matters, care proceedings and domestic abuse. Under the new rules, legal aid will be limited, to low income applicants (on benefits or means tested), but only if their situation falls into one of these categories:

- **Cases where there has been domestic abuse**
  Children, financial matters and applications for injunctions where the applicant is, or has been, the victim of domestic violence. These involve cases where one party has hurt, abused or threatened the divorce applicant or the applicant's child, and even where the abuse does not form a relevant part of the case before the courts.

  Domestic violence is defined as 'any incident of threatening behaviour, violence or abuse (psychological, physical, sexual, financial or emotional) between adults who are or have been, intimate partners or family members, regardless of gender or sexuality'. As well as the physical aspects, the definition includes aspects of control e.g. preventing access to money or family/friend support networks and also verbal abuse, such as name calling.

  Evidence of this abuse will need to be provided, and can be in the form of a conviction or caution, injunctive order or undertaking, a finding of fact made by the court, letter con-

firming violence from the Local Authority, health care professionals, domestic violence refuge or MARAC.

- **Local authority child protection matters**
If the local authority has child protection concerns, parents, children and other interested adults will continue to be able to access legal aid.

- **Child abduction cases**
If there is a history of, or risk of, child abduction outside the UK, or a child has been unlawfully removed within the UK, legal aid may be available.

- **Forced marriage**
Anyone threatened or forced to marry against their will can apply for a Forced Marriage Protection Order.'

Save in child protection and child abduction cases, legal aid will not be available for individuals responding to a divorce application, unless the respondent is also a victim of domestic abuse.

According to figures from Citizens Advice, these changes mean that of the 250,000 cases of divorce and family breakdown that historically, received legal aid each year, only 40,000 cases will be eligible in future.

So for most, it is now a matter of pay or do it yourself. And this includes family disputes, including those awful problems of, who will have the children, what visiting or staying arrangements are there to be and how much should one parent pay towards the upkeep of the children. The help that many good attorneys have offered will not be available except on a pro bono basis. What sort of a socially responsible state can create such a situation? Lawyers from many of the ranks from top judges to legal executives know that when a person tries to be a so called 'litigant in person' – LiPs – in other words, to go to court to present their own case, they often create more difficulties for themselves and also for the courts than when an advocate with knowledge and experience of the court's rules, procedures and the legal principles and powers stands there to represent the litigant.

Roger Smith tells[39] that in Holland, the Dutch Legal Aid Board has produced an inter-based, user-oriented module that private practitioners can add to their own websites, which helps those thinking of divorce, to make up their minds and prepare their cases. He envisages such a relationship in this country, between solicitor and client.

This to be contrasted with a report[40] that 'commoditised' advice failed to cover the full extent of a civil claim for damages. A lower court had also criticised the use of questionnaire and standardised letters with little personal contact. No doubt the same will be said of such packages in family matters.

The buzz word is 'unbundling'. In divorce there is a suggestion that a client wanting a divorce, whether or not he can obtain legal aid (which is now virtually impossible), should carry out a part of the procedures himself. It is called 'unbundling'. A Law Society note explains that it is the provision 'of isolated or discrete events of legal assistance' under a partial retainer rather than a traditional full retainer. In other words, the client calls in the solicitor to get one bit of the process and then goes off and tries to take the next step himself. I can just imagine the mess. When things go wrong it will be the solicitor who has to sort it out. It will delay the divorce and probably cost the client a great deal more than if he obtained a package deal.

The poor spouse starts by paying a small fee to a solicitor to help him draft a divorce petition and then he himself sends it the court to start the process. He carries out such further step as he can manage and as soon as he hits a problem he goes back to a solicitor who helps with that step. Instead of one solicitor doing it all for him – a complete bundle – he gets it in bits. Unbundled! I can just imagine some of the inarticulate and in-

---

39 LSG 12 January 2015
40 LSG 6 May 2015

adequate clients who I acted for, carrying out anything at all by themselves.

The Legal Aid and Advice Act 1949, often described as 'one of the corner stones of the welfare state', established a scheme of legal aid, intended to provide practical equality before the law for those of 'moderate means' as well as for the poor. At its height, the scheme covered the majority of the adult population and, at a cost of about £2 bn annually, was, per capita, the world's most expensive. Successive governments became concerned that the cost was escalating.

Over decades, the ambit of the scheme was narrowed: payments to lawyers were allowed to fall behind market rates; in 2000, claims for personal injury were removed; finally the Legal Aid, Sentencing and Punishment of Offenders Act 2012 (LASPO) made parties in most family cases ineligible for legal aid. Since many parties cannot afford representation without legal aid, the number of LiPs coming before the courts has grown. There is a sense amongst the judiciary, that something should be done. Adam Taylor, a District Judge[41], explained that the judge might have to take over the cross-examination himself. Will the questioning by the LiP be insufficient to render a trial fair? Why should the judge try to order the Court Service to provide help when in fact and law, he has no power to do so? These are all unanswered questions.

The growth in LiPs had led to the President of the Family Division giving guidance as to how a judge was expected to deal with a LiP. You cannot get more serious than that and the Master of the Rolls, Lord Dyson, has said, that to cope with a high proportion of LiPs, the profession should be:

> 'prepared to change our way of conducting our litigation to make it more effective, and reduce costs and delays'[42]

---

41 LSG 13 October 2014
42 LSG 27 April 2015

Surely this is the tail wagging the dog?

As regards LiPs, there was also a report of a litigant who attacked his wife during family court proceedings, thus highlighting security concerns about more people appearing in court without lawyers.

Even the Law Society has weighed in. It has published guidance[43] that:

> 'You should communicate in a manner of which the court would approve, which includes treating LiPs with courtesy and in a way that any ordinary person would regard as fair and reasonable. This does not mean that you have to tolerate unacceptable behaviour from a LiP nor does it mean that a LiP has a right to expect you to respond immediately to their call or correspondence.'

In the meantime, the family justice minister pledges to create a countryside network of in-court advice centres for unrepresented people at a cost of £1.4m per year.[44] The money will go to the Personal Support units which already exist in the courts. But the enhanced service will provide additional work clinics, advice by phone and email, a person to manage the service and an appointed judge with particular responsibility for LiPs. As the family mediation service Resolution commented, it would only be a sticking plaster for a family justice system wounded by cuts to legal aid.

I have also heard that some family disputes might be heard by a form of video conferences, described as 'rulings by Skype in online courts'.

Is this work now a trade or a profession? I argue a clear belief that it was and should remain, work for the Common Attorney. This is the very opposite to what is actually happening to the help that professionals are able to give. It is work which

---

43 LSG 8 June 2015
44 LSG 27 October 2014

is either complex and requires someone with an understanding of finance or alternatively, it requires someone with dedication and understanding.

It is suggested that mediation, as opposed to litigation, is the answer but mediation has been developing in such a way that it also needs the help and intervention of a representative and the mediator cannot guide and help support and sympathise. It is not the way forward that family disputes require.

I would rate this as a disaster for Joe Public. I also suggest that it is more of a disaster for little Jane public and little Joey public. The fact that Legal Aid is not available for the people engaged in divorce and is rarely available for issues relating to children is so unfair, it is verging on being a social disaster. I have picked out a few comments about the changes.

It is said that 6 out of 10 domestic violence victims are unable to get access to Legal Aid according to a survey by women's rights charities. Two surveys of 377 victims between 1st April and 31st July 2013 showed 61% of the women who had experienced, or were experiencing domestic violence, took no action in the family Court, because they were unable to apply for Legal Aid. Of the rest, 28% paid a solicitor privately and 16% represented themselves.

The Law Society Gazette[45] recorded that the percentage of domestic abuse victims who took no action, in relation to their family problem, as a result of not being able to apply for legal aid was 47 %.

On the other hand, a judge, Sir Paul Coleridge, called for an in independent commission to take a 'new and fresh' look at the divorce laws which had been unchanged for 40 years. He said that family law should reflect how life is lived now, not in the distant past. And he called for the profession to take the lead in developing more innovative and daring alternatives to the 'bloodshed, time and cost, of court'.

---

45 LSG 7 April 2014

Local courts have closed and from April 2014, the Single Family Court will be a national court for all family proceedings in England and Wales, and family cases will no longer be heard by the County Court or the Family Proceedings Court. So successful is the organisation that it made errors in calculating the financial settlement between couples and 2,235 of the cases will require a further application to the court to reopen or renegotiate different divorce settlements.[46]

A family judge lambasted the 'almost impenetrable' level of bureaucracy faced by solicitors, dealing with the Legal Aid Agency. He was reported in the Law Society Gazette[47] when referring to a case where a judge had made an order for up to £2,500 to be spent on a report from an expert in Indian family law. The Legal Aid Agency refused to grant authority for that arrangement and in the absence of any evidence, the judge had to make what appears to be an unsatisfactory order.

Perhaps the worst possible statistic or statement is a headline in the Times[48] 'Law students to help couples through divorce'. It has been the practice for a long period of time that persons engaged in claims before employment tribunals and similar tribunals, were able to use law students to assist them and even be their advocates. In my opinion, it is a step too far, for people whose marriages have broken down, whose family assets need to be sorted out, whose family relationships and emotional states are fragile, to have do obtain help from unqualified persons. Just imagine what would happen if it was decided that neither doctors nor nurses would look after patients in hospitals, or that surgeries would be done by students who have not yet even passed their examinations. Imagine if operations might be carried out by students, who are just learning surgery. Is it the type of work for professionals? Clearly a resounding 'yes' and that is an answer

---

46 LSG 1 February 2016
47 LSG 17th March 2014
48 22 April 2014

which is the very opposite to what is actually happening to the help that professionals were able to give in Family cases.

So is it good for the common attorney? The answer is the usual classic 'yes and no'. For the specialist who attracts the monied parties, it is a bonanza. They ask a multitude of questions to search for hidden assets or to find what they or the forensic accountant, who they retain, think is the true value of certain assets, such as pension funds or shares in private companies, especially a company which is nothing more than the family business. Those lawyers are in my opinion, all that is wrong in the profession, because so many of them seem to take their work to an extreme, but it is hard to criticise them. In the first place there are known cases where the asset rich spouse has done his or her utmost to mislead the other, but he or she forgets that when they slept together, there was enough pillow talk for some of the financial dodges to be discussed openly. The other spouse is like the elephant who did not forget! Secondly, the law seems to be in a constant state of flux. At one time, it was said that the wife was entitled to one third of the pot; then that she needed enough to maintain her lifestyle as had been during the marriage; then again, it is about parity or some other indefinable entitlement. It is due for yet further changes.

I come down on the side of saying that the changes in funding have been a disaster for the dedicated practitioner. I agree with Sir Paul Coleridge about a 'new and fresh look' at divorce law, but I contend that in this branch of the law, above all others, the government and everyone involved should recognise that the legal contribution to family health is in every way as important to the public as is the National Health Service.

I must add a footnote that may prove that many of my concerns may transpire to be unwarranted but for unexpected reasons. The Times[49] reports that divorce 'centers' will open throughout England and Wales where couples will be able to end their marriages over the counter. So you will not need lawyers at all.

---

49 22 June 2015

CHAPTER 7

A CRIMINAL LAWYER
[OR MORE ACCURATELY A CRIMINAL LAW PRACTITIONER]

Any lawyer who has ever practisedd in the criminal courts is always good value for money at a dinner party or in the pub. We all have stories to tell and the fact that you have had the responsibility for another man's future gives one the experience of fulfilling a duty. We have seen storytellers in court (in the nicest way). We have all been asked the question "How can you act for a man who you know is guilty?" And I hope that every lawyer can say "I never did." You are there as the advocate to put a man's case better than he can do himself. You develop a sense of when a man is going to say something to you, which means that if he goes on, he will ask you to tell a lie on his behalf. The experienced advocate never lets that point arrive. He develops a skill of stopping a client ever going that far. If he fails, then he cannot act any longer, unless the client pleads guilty. I had a case where a man said words to the effect of "I did it but they can't prove it." I immediately told him that I could not act any longer and sent him to another solicitor and advised him not to say anything so stupid. Later I learned from the other solicitor that he had been acquitted.

Before I qualified, I never thought that I would ever even appear in a magistrate's court – especially as an advocate. At one time, magistrate's courts were also known colloquially as police courts. My articles did not qualify me for that type of work. I think that in the five years of articles, my principal took on one criminal case. I think that it was a shop lifting plea of guilty for a family friend and he ensured that another articled clerk and I were there in court, although I don't think that either of us actually learned anything.

I have a recollection that as I was leaving the army, one of my squaddies asked me to defend him on a charge of indecent assault, at a hearing in a magistrate's court near Farnborough. I don't know whether it was because I was so bad or because I appeared in uniform, that the clerk asked if I was qualified. I assume that my client was convicted.

Soon after I started in practice in Leeds as an assistant solicitor, and was paid the measly sum of £15 a week. I remember appearing in the magistrate's court on a bail application. I did not even know the procedure or the criteria, but the occasion was memorable because for the first time, I heard Jack Levi, the best criminal solicitor advocate that I have ever known. He asked his questions in such a way that he forced the witness – an experienced police officer – to concede the points that he wanted to establish.

I did have some interesting cases and some which are worth recording. I never became a really top specialised criminal lawyer, although I remember sitting next to a judge at a dinner, many years ago, when he said to me "I hear that you are a heavy weight in court." It ought to go down as one of my most recordable moments! Although I was a general practitioner, I might have made more of a mark, if it had not been for the fact that things were changing in this field earlier and more rapidly, than they eventually did in other fields of law.

My first Quarter Sessions[50], case which still makes me smile, was the very nice chap who owned a small shoe shop. He was offered a large consignment of shoes at an extremely bargain price. He was to meet the sellers not in a warehouse, but in a remote location outside the town. When he met a couple of chaps, they told him to follow them to the pickup point for the goods. It was only when he found himself in the backyard of a police station that he realised, that was actually trying to buy some stolen goods. That was his defence to a charge of receiving. He was acquitted largely due to a very able barrister, the same E John Parris that I have quoted earlier.

---

50 Quarter Sessions are now the Crown Court

For instance, the idea of the old style committals for trial in which the clerk slowly typed the evidence as a deposition which was signed and used in the Assizes or Quarter Sessions went out of the window. In addition, there was a new rule, that in these early stages, the cases could not be reported in the press, except to state the name of the accused, the offence and a few other details, unless the defendant raised reporting restrictions. The old style practitioners like Jack Levi either did not like the new system or they felt that to make the details of the case public was not in the client's interest. A contemporary of mine, had a different approach. As there was no old style committal, it meant that he could do ten or more short committals in a morning. Whilst most other cases went unreported he raised reporting restrictions many times daily, with the result that he seemed to be the solicitor with most cases and thus, the reading public may have concluded, the best. I did not follow his example and I suppose that I fell behind – as did most of us including luminaries such as Jack Levi.

Nevertheless, my criminal practice grew gradually. I remember doing a small fraud case in Pontefract. It was something about selling advertising that was not published. I think that the Fraud Squad were impressed. Then I defended one client on an estate agency fraud. I briefed the great local Q.C., Rudolph Lyons. I sent him a very long brief and a very, very long proof of evidence. A few days before the hearing, he said that it would be more helpful to him if the proof was in a different order. I mobilised my secretarial staff and we produced the revised version overnight. He was most impressed. I then had a 'run' of fraudsters. It was one of those who told me that when in Armley he had a wonderful life. The walls of his cells, he said, were papered with pound notes and he peeled them off to bribe the warders who supplied him with good quality steaks.

At one time, it was quite reasonable for a solicitor to have a friendship or a working relationship with policemen, the press or even the magistrates' clerks and, believe it or not, even magistrates. I recollect that there was one nearby town in which, if you were appearing in the magistrates' court and there was a break for coffee, you were invited to have coffee with the magistrates.

There was a small town nearby, where at lunchtime, you were even asked in to have lunch with them. You knew the limits. You did not discuss work or cases. You made small talk, but it was pleasant and civilised. There was mutual respect and understanding.

There was a local public house where on Friday evenings, after work, all sorts of people who had been working in the courts just over the road would join together for a drink. There were magistrates' clerks, the press, the police, barristers and solicitors. We all treated one another equally. No one thought that there was anything wrong with this practice. I could imagine today that the press would immediately suggest there was some conspiracy between either the police and the solicitor or the magistrates' clerk. Professional life was pleasant in those days but I guess that such an atmosphere does not exist today.

The Fraud Squad started to have an annual dinner. I was the only solicitor invited to the first few. There were barristers, some who were Q.C.s, revenue officials, magistrate's clerks, and accountants and so on. The first time, I invited them home afterwards and served them vintage brandy from my collection. This became an institution and they came back for several years. Although it helped my image and standing, I know that my wife hated it, because you can imagine the noise that twenty or so large men would make after a few drinks. It kept her awake but it was in a good cause.

So now for the ruminations of an old lawyer.

I also had a run of clients who were known as the 'prop boys'. Leeds became infamous for them because although based in Leeds they operated all over the country. They were men with no scruples. Their technique was that, allegedly, they went to an old person's house and said that the roof needed repair and that they would like to inspect it and give an estimate. One kept the old person talking, the other said that he was going to look round, to work out what needed doing. They stole anything that was valuable and left. It was a particularly reprehensible type of crime.

The police got wise to them and the Regional Crime Squad would have a fleet of cars which took it in turn to follow them out of Leeds and to their destination and sometimes caught them in the act. The Regional Crime Squad were really hard men and they became convinced that my partner and I were accessories to these men. I believe that we were on their 'wanted' list. I remember that, after being given the run around all night, at Gipton police station, one of them, an Inspector, said to me that they were sure that one of the crooks had stolen a valuable stamp collection. He suggested that if it was in my safe (which it was not) and if I handed it over, they would be grateful and not take any action against me. I was furious and said so. They gave both my partner and me a hard time and we constantly felt the pressure. Our view was that we would do our best for our clients, but the police often think that if you work hard, then you have an ulterior motive – that you are part of the gang. I even learned that they had told the Chief Constable or some such person of their belief and he spoke to someone from the Fraud Squad who, fortunately, gave me a clean bill of health.

Possibly the pressure lessened after that, or perhaps it was something different altogether. On one occasion, the Regional Crime Squad head, an Inspector, said something to the effect that he knew that there were wonderful Law Society formal dinners and he had always wanted to attend one. One of his sergeants, a Scotsman, also expressed a similar wish. I checked with a senior officer in the police and with the Law Society, that it was okay and duly made them part of a large party. By way of reciprocation, the Scotsman asked my wife and me to a couple of ceilidhs, a Burns Night Dinner, which I found fabulous, and then to a Hogmanay Ceilidh. They were marvellous, as much because of the company as the actual event. People in the party included a well known artist, a TV producer, a vet and others. I used to look forward to the events until one year when we went back to the house of a policeman for first footing[51]. My wife came over

---

51 First footing is a northern and a Scottish tradition when the new year is greeted by the first person over the door step and who brings some sugar and coal

to me from the hall and insisted that we leave straight away. At first, I thought that someone had propositioned her, but she told me our host had been telling her how he achieved some of his successes. He said that he always carried a small envelope of cannabis and if he had difficulty with suspects, he would slip it into their pocket and claim that he could then arrest them for possession of drugs. My wife was so disgusted that I doubt if she has ever trusted the police again. We never went back to a ceilidh or a first footing!

I have been able to help a number of other solicitors, when they have been in trouble. One incident, relating to criminal law, arose out of those matters. Mr. M had been reported for attempting to pervert the course of justice. He had been called to a police station to represent a boy and advise him. The boy's parents for some reason reported that Mr. M had advised him to lie and they informed the police. He was asked to attend for interview by a very senior officer and he asked me to accompany him. We went to police HQ and as we were walking along one of the carpeted corridors (which shows how senior was the officer), a door opened and a man appeared and saw my client and said words to the effect of "John, what are you doing here?" They chatted without really answering him. As I stood there, I felt a strong sense of hostility from this chap so I said "I don't know who you are, but I feel that you don't like me." He replied "I'm Chief Superintendent X and I remember you Mr. Pearlman. Ten years ago in the Stipendiary Magistrates Court you called me a liar." and he shut his door with a bang. They say that an elephant never forgets but perhaps they should say the same about policemen.

There was another occasion when I was at the city's main police station and as I left, I got in a lift. There was a chap there already who I recognised as someone who had been a sergeant in the Regional Crime Squad, years earlier and with whom I had had trouble. As soon as the lift door closed, he said to me "I'll get you one day, Mr. Pearlman." I was genuinely worried, because it is not impossible for a policeman to manufacture evidence, so I wrote to the Chief Constable of West Yorkshire and recorded exactly what had happened and asked him to keep it on file in case this chap ever tried to 'fit me up'. Of course, he never did.

If I started to tell about my murder cases I would call it 'Most of my Murders' but I would then have stolen this title from an autobiographical volume by the same E. John Parris that I have already mentioned. I conducted three murder cases and I can boast that there was an acquittal in each of them but my most frequently told incident was not actually about one of those three cases.

My first client on a murder charge killed his girlfriend by strangling her with a cord. He said that there was trouble between them and he was so upset and could not remember what he had done but he accepted that he had killed her. A Q.C. defended him and on his advice, the client pleaded diminished responsibility[52]. The Q.C. told me that he had never before succeeded with that plea, but he did so on this occasion. The only noteworthy part of the story was that, when I was conducting the committal in the magistrate's court, my client asked me if he could go to the loo and I asked for a short adjournment. I went, he went handcuffed to his jailers and as I stood there I realised that he, I, the jailers, the clerk of the court *and the magistrates were all standing there in a row in the loo!*

The next case was a man who killed his mother but he was a drug addict and was so drugged up that he did not know what he was doing. Also diminished responsibility. The third had hit out at his girlfriend's small child in simple irritation and managed to hit her hard in the stomach. The child choked on her vomit. He admitted manslaughter which the prosecution accepted and he was put on probation. Now there are sentencing guidelines and he would most likely have been sentenced to six years imprisonment.

---

52 Where a person kills ... he shall not be convicted of murder if he was suffering from such abnormality of mind ... as substantially impaired his mental responsibility for his acts or omissions in doing so ... Section 2 Homicide Act 1957.

The other murder case, in which I had some involvement, was that of a client of my partner, but it is the murder which I most frequently mention. I think that the man was well known as being extremely violent. He was arrested on suspicion of having killed a tailor, probably in the course of theft. It was on a Friday night and my partner was away. I dealt with the interviews and then decided that I wanted information about the autopsy. The rule was that the Home Office pathologist was obliged to share his findings with the defence and a friend of mine happened to be the pathologist. I phoned him and he asked me to go round on Sunday lunchtime. When I got there, the family were just sitting down to lunch. He was carving a leg of lamb. He passed the gory post mortem photos round the table and his children, aged then about 8 and 10, looked at them in a quite unconcerned way and went on eating. I watched him carve and thought, that is exactly what you have just done to a human body. My partner was back on Monday morning so that was the end of my involvement in the case. The 'perp' was convicted of murder.

One of my favourite cases was what I called the 'Porn Shirt' case. A client had a small clothing shop mainly selling T shirts, on which were printed various pictures and messages, which on one possible interpretation, were quite rude, but in an obscure way. He was charged with obscenity. I took into court by way of comparison, a T shirt which I had bought that looked as though it was written in Hebrew. However, if you could see the mirror image it said something very rude in stylised English such as 'F...you'. He was acquitted!

I had a client [L] who pleaded guilty to be acquitted! He had come up with the idea that if he befriended a chap who worked at the Mecca ballroom, he could borrow the safe key, have a copy made and then return and take the contents of the safe. He duly received the key and went to a local key cutter and asked for a copy. Unknown to him, the key cutter was suspicious and called the police who were there waiting for him and on arrival arrested him. Eventually, at the Quarter Sessions, he pleaded guilty to conspiracy with the ballroom employee so he was sent to the cells, to await sentence. His co-accused, pleaded not guilty and after a trial, was acquitted. In those days it was usual for the indictment to name the co-conspirator. So my client had to be re-arraigned and he changed his plea and was set free. There was an unusual moment in the trial. One of the prosecution witnesses was Jimmy Saville, whose only claim to fame in those days was that he was the manager of the Mecca Ballroom. He was very late for court and the judge, Henry Scott, was furious. Then he turned up with hair dyed white, which caused a sensation! That was one of two occasions when I met the man who, for years, was looked upon as one of our greatest local heroes but who now is reviled. Perhaps it was my good fortunes that our paths crossed so rarely.

That same client [L] deserves a special extra mention. He was a thief, but more intelligent than the average punter I had got him off several charges and then he was convicted of a charge of receiving and sent to jail. I went down to the cells after the trial and he said "Honestly, Mr. P, I was innocent this time. Those other times when I got off I was guilty so I can't complain."

On 8th March 1971, I had three successful cases in the magistrate's court. I remember one was a chap who had used foreign coins in a parking machine and it was claimed to be a fraud, but he said it was an accidental mixing of coins on return from abroad. Another, was a woman shop lifter, but I cannot remember the other, except that it was a motoring case. Really a most memorable, but singular, day!

You meet some funny characters in general legal practice. CC was a West Indian who had a happy-go-lucky attitude to life and actually was thoroughly irresponsible. He was ruthless as well. He would not observe the law or its principles.

He ran a shabeen (an unlicensed illegal drinking den) in Chapeltown. He had no licence, but I think that at that time, the police were working on the basis that it was better to turn a blind eye to these establishments to avoid racial trouble. CC was also a pimp for a prostitute who had several convictions for prostitution and it was clear that the next one would result in her being sent to prison. She was charged with importuning on Grange Avenue, in the middle of Chapeltown (of all places). The police said that they had observed her, from round the corner. She said that she was not guilty and explained that, even if she had been on the street, the police could not have seen her, because the place where they said that they had carried out their observations was behind a thick hedge and it obscured any view. That was to be her defence. A few days before the trial date, I realised that she had not been in touch to give me full instructions, although I had tried to contact her. I decided to make a site visit to find out if there was any merit in the defence and whether the hedge was thick enough to stop the police observing her.

I did not like the idea of visiting a prostitute's residence alone, so I arranged for a partner to accompany me. CC answered the door and invited us in, to a ground floor living room and told us that she had gone 'on the run'. We left and when we were in the car, I said to my partner "Did you see the whips?" There had been a selection of whips on the delft rack! (Presumably for bondage sessions!) He had not noticed them!

CC also caused me some humour. I went to defend him in Wolverhampton and all of a sudden, there was some challenge, as to whether or not he could have been in a particular place. He suddenly produced an alibi (I should mention that this was before the days when you had to give notice of an alibi). He produced an appointment card for an STD clinic, showing that he had an appointment there at that time and date!

I had a client on a criminal charge of an offence in London and he was to appear at the Old Bailey. It was my one and only Old Bailey case. He was pleading guilty, but I brought in a psychiatrist, who took the view that the guy's previous life had an effect on him but he was now treating him and he was convinced that he would go straight ... or something like that. He got a suspended sentence. Later, I was talking to Jack Levi, the greatest solicitor criminal advocate I ever knew, who told me that in his long career, he only had one case at the Old Bailey. I felt good.

Of course there was always a danger that, your criminal client saw you as one of his team and from time to time, one reads in the papers about the lawyer who becomes the rogue or the accessory, as in the Great Train Robbery case. One client tried it on me. I had been representing a man on a fraud charge, I had represented him earlier, on at least one other fraud. He went 'on the run', in other words, he ran away abroad, in breach of his bail conditions and could not be found. A year or so later I received a phone call from someone, telling me that he was from New Scotland Yard and wanted to come north to meet me. Puzzling and worrying! He showed me a photograph of a man with dark glasses and asked if I recognised him. Upon my denial, he showed me the back of the photo and there was my name, but not my handwriting and it suggested that I had signed to confirm his visual identity, in order to obtain a fraudulent passport. My own client had tried to use me. When he eventually returned to England, I refused to act for him on the good reason that I might be called as a witness against him!

There are many debates about the powers of the police, or other investigatory authorities, but I am convinced that, despite many protestations to the contrary, there must have been a fairly regular practice of tapping or otherwise intercepting phones. I was acting for a solicitor, who had been in trouble with the police, but had been acquitted. He came to see me again, because the investigating police officers were making further enquiries and it looked as though they were disappointed that their original allegations had been unfounded. It looked as though they were now pursuing a vendetta. He had phoned me to make an appointment to see me and whilst he was with me, I decided to phone the officers to ask them to explain themselves. I lifted my phone and as I dialled the first digit, I found that I had what is usually called, a crossed line. It was with the very police station to which the officers were attached. It was too much of a coincidence.

There was another separate occasion, but not one where I was in any way acting as a lawyer. I happened to be an officer of the Ramblers Association and there was controversy about a public footpath, which ran across a local American air force base, but which was obstructed by a high security fence. I telephoned a colleague to arrange a site visit one Sunday morning. We arrived and parked on the roadside verge, where the path started. Within just one minute, a police car arrived. The policeman came over and said "Mr. Pearlman, what are you doing here?" I did not know him but he clearly knew that I was coming. How else could he have known, unless someone had heard us making our arrangements to visit?

The police can act on reasonable suspicion, but they can be led to a false conclusion by the unexpected. I had a client who had made good. He had probably been a juvenile delinquent, but he learned how to make money honestly, but was not a conformer. He had just split up with his wife and so bought a very small house in a rundown area of town … but he drove a Rolls Royce! He parked it outside the house. He had not bothered to furnish the house in a conventional manner and was quite content to sleep on a mattress on the floor. The police were suspicious – probably alerted by neighbours. They raided the house and arrested him. I was called one evening when I was about to go to a formal dinner, so I was in a dinner jacket. What a sight … a rather unkempt man and his formally dressed solicitor, telling the police that to park a Roller in a rundown area of town was not a crime. They said that they were going to search the house, even under the floor boards, but they found nothing and had to release him. To be honest, it was hilarious, especially as the client treated the whole thing, even arrest and search, as a big joke.

The normal oath given by a witness, is to tell the truth, the whole truth and nothing but the truth. I was rarely a witness in court but I once experienced how an otherwise honest witness did not tell the whole truth. My client [D] ran what seemed a successful and normal business. He asked me to join him for lunch to introduce me to his new bank manager. I discovered that he was changing his accountants, as well as his bank, so together with one of his partners, it was quite a big gathering. I rarely drank alcohol at lunchtime, but as the wine flowed, I joined in, as did the bank manager. It ended fairly late, but only after my client had bribed the head waiter, with a £50 note to serve champagne, after the then licensing hours. Years later, the client was facing a charge of fraud on the bank and I read the statement of that bank manager. It read something like 'On 18th June had a meeting with Mr. D...' No mention of the lunch and definitely no whole truth about the drinking.

Things have changed and although Joe Public probably thinks that the police and the courts are much the same, as they were forty years ago, I find the criminal process almost unrecognisable.

The most important single change, was the Police and Criminal Evidence Act 1984 (PACE) which led to taped interviews; the attendance of a solicitor at the interview: the extra formalities of cautioning a suspect before questioning; rules about identification procedures and about giving advanced notice of an alibi. There are also many more opportunities for forensic and other scientific procedures, which can be used to track down and help convict wrongdoers.

But what the public do not know, is that there may be more or less, or the same amount of crime, as years ago, but there are far, far fewer cases, coming before the courts. In recent years, due to reasons such as financial constraints, overwork, fewer active officers or whatever, the police charge fewer offenders. They prefer to offer a caution, which many offenders will accept, to avoid the risk of going to court and possibly being sent to prison or fined. This meant less time spent on paper work for the policeman

A retiring Crown Court judge was reported as alleging[53] that the police forces were 'massaging' crime figures, by preventing cases from going to court, to save officer's time. In a scathing attack, upon the criminal justice system, he said:

> "The figures have been massaged. Robbery is now classified as theft from a person: burglary is downgraded to criminal damage. Cautions and reprimands are used to save police time. But you ask the people who walk about

---

53 Times 18 April 2014

the towns and cities at night if crime has gone down and they will give you a very different picture."

He claimed that the government had forced him to pass sentences that were too lenient, and that initiatives such as suspended sentences, had failed.

"Sentencing is a skill only acquired after long experience and cannot be reduced to a tick in a box. We've had suspended sentences introduced, abolished then introduced again. All this tinkering about is more to do with money and votes, rather than criminal justice while the prison population has continued to rise. None of the government initiatives have worked. We've now got warnings, reprimands, cautions, conditional discharges that prevent people from appearing in court."

The government regularly and loudly complains about the amount earned by advocates and little by little, is reducing the amount paid for legal aid, in criminal cases. The government seems convinced that lawyers are milking the system. They seem to feel that a good lawyer, an experienced Queen's Counsel who practisess criminal law and deals with very serious and complex cases such as murder, rape and fraud is being paid too much for his services Even the judges criticise the Q.C.s, although they themselves were in that very position only a few years earlier. (This seems to be a mindset of many barristers and former barristers! They seem to forget their past once they ascend the bench.)

It is true that a case in the Crown Court can generate a huge number of many complex facts, such as the scientific evidence and they generate an enormous amount of paper which the advocate has to spend hours reading, analysing and preparing the way of questioning it. Strangely, although the prosecution is under an obligation to produce unused material, if the advocate reads it (as a cautious advocate would) he is not allowed to charge for his time doing so.

If a surgeon was to spend a similar amount of time preparing for and carrying out, a similarly complex operation, no one, least of all the government, would complain. But lawyers are to be treated differently!!

Crime is not what it was! I write as a solicitor and not a criminal. Many solicitors cut their advocacy teeth on minor appearances in the magistrate's court. One learned the ways of the courts. There is nothing better than to be trying to convince court, whilst you are standing on your feet. Young solicitors rarely have the opportunity to fight a contested case as an advocate. As you would expect, the more elderly solicitors say that 'the present lot are not as good as our lot!'

As regards the availability of legal aid, for criminal cases, the position is different to that for matrimonial and civil matters. According to the web site of FindLawUk:

'If you are taken to a police station and interviewed under caution or arrested, you are entitled to free legal advice regardless of your financial situation.

Legal aid at court
To apply for legal aid at court, you will automatically qualify if you:
- are under 18
- receive specific state benefits, which are:
- income support
- income-based job seeker's allowance
- guaranteed state pension credit
- income-related employment and support allowance

If these do not apply to you, you may apply for legal aid at court but your case will be subject to the 'interests of justice' test, which considers the merits of your case, and you will be subject to a means test to determine your financial position.

Interests of Justice

The interests of justice test looks at how serious your case is: if you have been charged with an indictable only offence (one that will be heard in the Crown Court) your case will pass the test. However, if you have been charged with a non-imprisonable offence, your case will not pass.

Means Test

The means test will look at how much income you receive and how much capital (such as savings or a house) you own. If your annual income is less than £12,475, you will be able to receive criminal legal aid.'

The future is becoming the present, as illustrated by the following, which appeared on the Law Society website[54]:

'Commenting on the development (the closure of Criminal defence firm, Carneys Solicitors of Leicester), the Law Society's head of legal aid, Richard Miller said: "This news, coming hot on the heels of the news about Challinors (another closed criminal firm), serves to underline the point we have been making to the Ministry of Justice, that firms undertaking criminal legal aid, are economically vulnerable – even at current rates of remuneration." "If the ministry insists on cutting rates still further, then regardless of any restructuring of the market, it will be taking a significant risk of accelerating the collapse of its supplier base," he added.

The government has established a tender process for duty solicitor contracts which will result in the reduction of criminal legal aid contracts from around 1600 to 527. It is claimed[55] that hun-

---

54 6 August 2013
55 LSG 30 March 2015

dreds of firms could go out of business, now that the government's plans have come into effect, after an unsuccessful court challenge by the law associations. The fact that a solicitor is paid so little, for spending a day or two in the magistrates court, fighting a case, leads to him advising his client to elect to go to a higher court (if the offence is one which allows him that choice) or he brings in a barrister. He might even advise him to plead guilty.

The new Criminal Legal Aid (General) Regulations 2013 came into force on 1 April 2013. There are a limited number of firms of solicitors which are allowed to carry out criminal legal aid (the contract) so that the client no longer has a free choice of representation. Even if he chooses a franchised solicitor, he may have to move if there is already another such lawyer acting for a co-accused provided that there is no conflict.

The fees paid are derisory and quite ridiculous. There are two fixed fees for magistrates' court trials. The lower fixed fee for a trial (any class) is £313.23. To qualify for the higher standard fee of £653.99, solicitors must do a minimum of core costs of £422.96. These include preparation, advocacy, sending attendance letters and phone calls. In metropolitan areas, such as Manchester, it does not include travel or waiting time at court (which could be hours). In January 2016, the government intends to replace the two fees, with one fee of £449.45. With other costs, such as overheads, office costs, IT, salaries, ongoing training and indemnity insurance to consider, firms are operating under considerable pressure.[56]

Imagine a surgeon being paid that amount for an operation and having to pay the amount charged by the hospital for staff and equipment and materials and his anesthetist. The lawyer has to pay all the costs of running his office.

It is little wonder that some members of the profession have gone on strike or a type of work to rule. Solicitors in Manchester started to boycott new legal aid work from 1 July; the Crim-

---

56 LSG 20 July 2015

inal Bar Association voted in favour of no new (legal aid) work and 'no returns' (meaning that when one barrister found that he could not attend a case it should be conducted by a second at short notice); solicitors are considering withdrawing from the duty solicitor scheme.

The effect so far has attracted the following examples which are likely to the first of many. Nearly 24 hours and 89 phone calls were required to find a solicitor to represent a police station detainee.[57] The ... day was described as 'horrendous' by one member of the court staff, with 34 people in custody and only two duty solicitors. Unrepresented defendants were being taken up, only to be taken back to the cells, because their case was too serious.[58] My local legal newssheet suggests[59] that the legal aid cuts threaten 160 firms in Yorkshire and the North east. Amazingly, the Government backed down, and the Times reported:[60]

'At the same time as stopping the lowering of fees, the justice secretary announced that he was abandoning a proposed system of contracts for which solicitors would have been forced to bid to do legal aid work in police stations.'

What is the opposite of a 'double whammy'? I am tempted to say that common sense has prevailed, but I fear that there is probably worse in the pipeline.

What a dilemma – for solicitors, for defendants and for the courts. But apparently, not for the government.

The moral is – don't commit crime! Or for the lawyer – don't be a criminal lawyer!

What I find even worse, is the way in which legal aid is now administered. Joe Public cannot go to the solicitor of his choice,

---

57 LSG 13 July 2015
58 LSG 20 July 2015
59 Leeds and Yorkshire Lawyer Issue 135 September 2015
60 29 January 2016

when he is in trouble with the police. Many solicitors are not able to do any work under the Legal Aid Administration. There is now a system of tendering for legal aid work. A solicitor has to convince the Legal Aid Agency that he is capable of doing legal aid work, in the magistrates court, or even the Crown Court. He is on a list and will be assigned by way of tendering to conduct a certain number of legal aid cases per year.

Even if the solicitor does continue to work, as a criminal practitioner, he is not necessarily, properly compensated. For instance, there are now fixed fees and if a solicitor finds that he is dealing with a case that requires a considerable amount of time this does not mean that he will be paid any extra. Can you imagine a doctor who is only allowed to spend a short amount of time with a patient and then has to say to him "No. Go away I cannot help you to stop the pain, because I am only allowed to listen to you but cannot recommend any treatment for you." The charging rate which was allowed for criminal cases has already been reduced by 8.75 % and a further 8.75% reduction is on the way.

The opportunities for gaining experience by taking part in a contested case are now lessened. This has come about by an unusual route. In March 2015, the rules were changed so that a defendant, who fought a case, but was found guilty would have to pay court costs of £520, irrespective of his financial ability to pay. This clearly results in an incentive to exit the process early, by the only means possible – a guilty plea.

A recent twist in the tail, was the introduction by the Ministry of Justice (some are calling it the Ministry of Injustice) of fixed costs, which must be paid by a defendant in the criminal court. In the magistrates' courts, a defendant convicted on a guilty plea, must pay £150 but must pay £520, if convicted after a trial. In the Crown Court, a conviction on a guilty plea attracts a fee of £900 and if convicted at a trial, on indictment, the fee is £1200. More reports are appearing of people who are innocent, but who plead guilty to avoid the increased fee, It has led to dozens of magistrates quitting because of what they see as unfair and illogical criminal court charges.[61] Not only will this lead to less work for the criminal practitioner, but when they have acted for someone, who later claims to have been innocent, but pleaded guilty for the wrong reason, the solicitor will certainly be blamed. For once, as they say, 'common sense prevailed' and the Minister for Justice abandoned the charge.

But there is another threat. That is the so called McKenzie Friend. He is an unqualified person who may be allowed by a court to act as an advocate for another person. They have been a rarity but now a so called watch dog, the Legal Services Consumer Panel says that they are a 'legitimate feature of the modern legal market' and improve access to justice.[62] They charge for their services, but have no professional structure or control. Is this to be the future? Is it to be the case that because the government restricts Legal Aid, then there will be a new group of people who allegedly fill the gap? First it will be the criminal courts then the divorce courts and the civil litigation courts. They have caused alarm bells to ring and the chairman of the Family Law Bar Association says 'they are cannibalising work that the bar should be doing'.[63] They have formed 'The Society of Professional McKenzie Friends' and say:

> 'Solicitors are too expensive for many people. [Those] who can't afford solicitors should have the option of a cheaper alternative. Part of that is driven by the costs of regulation and I have a lot of sympathy for solicitors but you have to look at the reality. The market has changed and people have to adapt'[64]

The cheek and the irony!

---

61 LSG 7 September 2015
62 LSG 28 April 2014
63 LSG 1 June 2105
64 LSG 10 November 2014

Their appearance has prompted the Law Society to issue guidance[65]. They stress that it is for the court or objecting party to provide sufficient reasons why a litigant should not receive assistance. However, a lawyer is entitled to raise concerns if they believe a McKenzie friend will not observe the confidentiality of proceedings, is being unreasonable, or is using the litigant as a 'puppet' to promote their own interests. And, more to the point perhaps:

> 'Lawyers should also flag up when they believe a McKenzie friend is charging more than a lawyer would, and should not communicate directly in court with a McKenzie friend.'

The idea that a Mackenzie friend should have a right of audience to represent people in a criminal court, is the scariest of all the ideas presently being floated. This is work for a professional who understand the law, the legal procedures, the investigatory procedures and who had a skill in analysing a case and putting it fairly and expertly to the court. Whilst it is still the field of a properly qualified lawyer it is definitely professional work. If the layman can take over, it demolishes the whole professionalism of the legal process. I hope that this is one of the terrible proposals that is quickly abandoned.

Perhaps crime is not as great a moral sin as it used to be. I was intrigued to read that Lord Justice Leveson is suggesting that 'low level offenders pleading guilty could be sentenced automatically and pay their fines by credit card.'

To add to the dramatic changes which have been effected so far, there is yet another new 'initiative'. The Lord Chancellor argues that he can liberate tens of thousands of individuals and free hundreds of hours of professional time. So he suggests that 'Online solutions and telephone and video hearings can make justice easier to access and reduce the need for long – and often

---

65 LSG 8 June 2105

multiple – journeys to court' Thus he continues 'we can reduce our dependence on an ageing and ailing court estate, which costs around one-third of the entire courts and tribunal budgets.'[66] I immediately remembered the closure of all those wonderful cottage hospitals and the loss of a truly local and personal source of medical help and advice. At least the health service provides an ambulance service to transport some patients to hospital. I will wager that no one will offer litigants a free taxi service to court.

All these changes have some good and some bad results.

Is it still work for the professional?

I am no longer practicing in the criminal courts and much of my view is influenced by conversations with others, who still do practice. I am told that senior solicitors are concerned that the standard of advocacy has diminished considerably. The more experienced older solicitors are doing a good job and they often appear in the Crown Court and I believe that judges consider that they are doing a good job. However, I am given to understand that young solicitors do not seem to have the opportunity to learn the trade of an advocate. They do not want to enter into contested cases requiring cross examination. In my day, one took every legal point that one could. I am given to understand that most advocates make the case as short and as speedy as possible. They do not feel that it is in their own interest, let alone the client's interest, to get involved in the major arguments over minor points of law. It is clearly work for the professional.

Is it good for Joe Public? All that I have so far described, means that the public is not properly protected. We all know that there are still cases of wrongful convictions. And how are people to be protected against such wrongful convictions, if there are not experienced solicitors, who are there at the right time and place with the right knowledge and skills to be able to protect people? I consider that this is an unmitigated disaster, for Joe Public. When I explained my view, to a regular criminal advocate, he

---

66 LSG 6 July 2015

expressed a completely different view. He considers that Joe Public gains, because he eventually will always be assigned a solicitor who is an expert. I maintain my view!! It did occur to me that as one who will obtain a contract, he can afford to adopt his view!!

Poor Joe Public. I hope that what I have already said has convinced you that it is bad. Very bad.

Poor Common Attorney. He is at the bottom of the pile and the pile is fading away.

CHAPTER 8
LITIGATION

'ELIZABETH THE SECOND by the Grace of God,
of the United Kingdom of Great Britain and Northern Ireland
and of Our other realms and territories Queen,
Head of the Commonwealth, Defender of the faith;

To Joe Blogs of 10 Greenacre, Sometown in the County of
Barsetshire We command you that within 14 days of the
service of this writ on you, inclusive of the day of service,
you do cause an appearance to be entered for you
in an action at the suite of Harry Barnfather.

WITNESS Lord Howsoever Lord Chancellor'

The words of the writ formerly used to
commence an action even for debt

Fighting another man's cause, is really what being a lawyer is all about. It is a reason why lawyers exist as a profession. They are doing for a client what the client cannot really do for himself, or perhaps do it so well. Of course, the client can decide to do it himself. He will find it rather like trying to cure his own illness, or carrying out an operation on himself, or extracting his own teeth. Sometimes, he might just get it right – choose the correct medicine or prick the right place but the law like medicine is necessarily complicated. It is complicated because men have made it so. It is the skill of the lawyer and his duty to his client, to look for ways of getting round the system or at best, look for another man with additional skills, such as a tax specialist, who will find a way for him. Every time the lawyer finds a way round, another lawyer, or even a politician, will try and make it harder for that route to continue. So, as one person finds a way to avoid being convicted of a crime, by using a technicality, the law tries to stop the gap and thus makes the law more complicated. Every time, a man finds a way of avoiding paying tax[67] and the government introduces new legislation to stop him, taxation becomes more and more labyrinthine, but tax specialists still try to find a way of avoiding tax. The classic example of how it works, is the many well known people and great international companies or wealthy individuals, in media or sport, who have earned vast sums of money but pay virtually no tax.

Lawyers always get the blame, but if you examine cases, you find that it is the specialist consultant or an accountant, who dreams up the complicated tax schemes. In many cases, it is the expert who thinks of unexpected explanations for injuries or failures to use the correct treatment; experts who explain how food, or machines or ships or airplanes should be manufactured, prepared or serviced; expert planners who can explain how the planning system should work and why the planning authority was wrong to deny planning permission. It is the lawyer who presents their findings and therefore when criticism is to be made, it is directed against the lawyer.

Lawyers are blamed for being the creators of the compensation culture. This is a culture that first came from the United States of America but it soon caught on here. To a certain degree, that was foreseeable, because it isn't fair that a large company can afford a lawyer whereas the customer or client could not. The introduction of Legal Aid with the Legal Aid Act of 1952 meant that many people then had the opportunity to instruct a lawyer to act for them in a claim. Perhaps it went a little too far, because there then developed a rule, to the effect that if a person was a legally aided litigant then even if he lost his case, there would not be an order for costs against him. Although it is

---

67 i.e. mitigation which is lawful compared with avoidance which is illegal

often criticised by the press, I wonder what is really wrong with the compensation culture. If something is wrong, why not complain and why not be compensated?

I had a lovely client whose wife had left him and who was looking after two young children. He came in telling me that he and the children were upset because a large dirty bandage had been found in a cereal packet. He brought the bandage as evidence. I wrote to the company which soon offered some compensation. About two years later, he came in with exactly the same complaint and it seemed to me, as though it was the same bandage. I told him in no uncertain terms, that if he tried it on again, it could be fraud and he could end up in jail. He decided that he did not need compensation that time.

Nevertheless, overall it was good that people were able to bring proceedings for many problems, such as accident claims, breach of contract or the supply of defective goods. They could also defend cases brought against them which were wrong or improper. At least it was like that but no longer is!

Originally, when one had a client who might qualify financially, for legal aid, you put a case to a committee of lawyers run by the Law Society who decided whether or not the client had a reasonable case. At the time I was able to obtain legal aid for one of my big cases about common land. It was deemed to be in the public interest. In fact, I even took it further and was able to obtain legal aid to complain that the Law Society had refused my client legal aid to bring another of his cases. That case went as far as the High Court and appeared in at least one law report.[68]

Since those days, the financial limits, which a proposed litigant must meet, have become more and more stringent. There is more money going to pay for medical treatment but less and less for legal help. Gradually, various types of legal work which formerly attracted legal aid or legal advice (the two being separate types of assistance) have become very limited.

---

68 R – v – No. 9 Legal Aid Area ex parte Bunting 1972

Other changes can be summarised as:

> A ban on referral fees
> Legal aid abolished except for neurological injuries caused during pregnancy, birth or in the first eight weeks after birth.
> Success fees are no longer recoverable from the losing side.
> Success fees up to 25% of damages, excluding damages for future care and lost which are protected in their entirety.
> Availability of damage based agreement as a means of funding cases.

It is becoming a matter of concern, that as a result of some of the changes, the courts now place administration as being more important than access to justice. It has now got to the stage where hardly anyone can get legal aid for anything other than some criminal work, with which I have dealt separately.

As explained in a government website, one might be able to get legal advice from Civil Legal Advice (CLA) if you qualify for legal aid and have problems with:
- debt, if your home is at risk
- housing
- domestic abuse
- family, if you've been in an abusive relationship
- special educational needs
- discrimination
- issues around a child being taken into care

To qualify for legal aid:
- your income (or combined income if you have a partner) shouldn't be more than £2,657 a month before tax
- your savings (or combined savings if you have a partner) shouldn't be more than £8,000

There are few people who actually qualify on this basis.

Unfortunately, there has been a completely separate development and that is the emergence of what some people called ambulance chasers. These are solicitors who actually set up a specialist service to claim compensation for certain types of injuries, especially those sustained in road traffic cases. They advertise on radio and TV and even on the back of buses. This has become a matter of political controversy and gradually, the government has intervened so that solicitors who are trying to help people, who are injured in road traffic cases are severely limited or even excluded, from the opportunity of getting reasonable remuneration for the work that they do.

As with everything else, it can go too far and as I explained, it developed the litigation culture. It has now gone too far the other way.

Of course, it is well known that some people fraudulently claim to be suffering from, for instance, whiplash when they have been in an accident. This meant that there were solicitors who were specialising in claims for whiplash. The government has now decided to restrict the amount that they are able to receive by way of costs for the work that they do. It has been stated that there were a substantial number of solicitors involved in road traffic accident litigation and this ruling, which has been supported by the High Court, is a severe blow to them.

An even more harmful curb is in the amount which the injured party can claim. The Chancellor of the Exchequer has announced banning general damages for soft tissue injuries and increasing the small-claims procedure limit, for all personal injury claims from £1000 to £5000, with effect from 2017.[69] This may be bad for the common attorney but it is just unbelievably bad for his client. It is the client who has suffered the injury and is (or claims to be) in pain. Why should he loose out? Apparently, it will save the insurance industry £1bn a year. My thought is, so what?

In the absence of legal aid, the ways in which litigation is funded can vary. First, there is the simple straightforward way –

---

69 LSG 30 November 2015

a solicitor takes on the case and is paid for his services according to either a fixed fee or according to the time he spends on the case. He can enter into what is called a conditional fee agreement, whereby he only gets paid if he wins. This also includes the possibility that he might be paid more if he is a specialist person winning the case. Many litigants find that they have insurance policies which enable them to instruct a solicitor, but the insurance company prefers the client to use the solicitor of its choice. There are now opportunities for after the event insurance (ATE) which attracts an unusually high premium, because there is great risk. The way in which litigation is funded is a nightmare, both for the practitioner and also for Joe Public.

The way in which the government proposes to regulate personal injury cases is that there will be a fixed fee payable, according to the amount of compensation that the client receives. As there has been such a scheme in existence for some time, it is said that the amount the solicitor will receive, has now been cut by almost 2/3. It is said that it will wipe £200 billion off the earnings of the solicitors who specialise in this type of work.

The fact that the government has intervened to try and regulate the manner, in which solicitors, try to earn a living from this branch of the law, demonstrates that something is or has been wrong and it is likely that some specialist practitioners have caused some public disquiet. So we have regulations that affect so called Claims Management Companies and restrictions on the payment of referral fees for personal injury cases, although it seems that other work is referred on a fee sharing basis. On the other hand, some barristers complain that solicitors are asking for part of the barrister's fee as a 'thank you' for giving him the brief. Do I sound pompous if I say that all this sounds distasteful? The chairman of the Bar Council (the barristers' trade union!) suggested that 'administration fees which some solicitors ask advocates to pay are just a cloak for 'referral fees"[70] and he

---

70 LSG 26 October 2015

earned a riposte from a solicitor saying[71] that it was a scandalous accusation and challenging the chairman to produce some evidence. I hope that no such evidence ever emerges.

I am told that the intervention also relates to After the Event insurance premiums and success fees. At the end of the day it seems as though both the client and the solicitor are losers. Especially with a change in the old rule, that the winner was granted an order that the loser pays his reasonable costs. Now with something called Qualified One-Way Costs Shifting the client is even worse off. I predict that this is one field where whatever is the rule today will be changed yet again tomorrow.

I have found the scene so confusing that I sought help from a colleague, who gave me the following explanation:

> 'Referral fees for personal injury were banned from 1 April 2013 under the Legal Aid, Sentencing and Punishment of Offenders Act 2012 (LASPO). However, they are still legal for other areas of work e.g. conveyancing.
>
> To replace referral fees in personal injury has come 'introduction fees'. What is the difference? With a referral fee, the Claims Management Company (CMC) contacted the Solicitor direct in respect of the Claimant's claim. With an 'introduction fee' the CMC gives the Claimant the Solicitor's details and asks the Claimant to contact the Solicitor direct. So politically, the Government were able to say they have done something about the compensation culture. In practice – nothing has changed
>
> Further, there is scope for a Solicitor's Firm and CMC(s) to form an ABS and get round the rules that way.
>
> Initially, motor insurers were able to shout there was a reduction in insurance premiums. The Solicitors found ways round the ban!

---

71 LSG 9 November 2015

When the Jackson reforms (see later) were introduced on 1 April 2013, claimants in general were able to get an extra 10% in damages. In practice, it is unclear of any significant uplift in damages

However, the biggest deduction from client damages for personal injury, is in respect of After The Event (ATE) insurance premium and success fees. Since 1 April 2013 ATE is not recoverable from the losing party and the success fee is payable from the winning party, rather than the losing party. The effect of this is that the Claimant's damages are severely reduced by these deductions.

There is a question whether or not the Claimant needs ATE. After 1 April 2013 QOCS came in – qualified one-way costs shifting. In general this means if you lose, you do not have to pay the other side's costs. However, there are some exceptions. Sceptics amongst us will say that the deduction from the Claimant's damages for ATE, is merely extra revenue for the Solicitor. ATE of over £400 for a road traffic accident are not unknown: the cost of the premium itself is much, much less.

Success fees in personal injury cases have been capped at 25% of the winner's costs – again a big deduction from the Claimant's damages.'

Try explaining that to a layman!

As a high street practitioner, I was involved in many and varied types of litigation. I used to say that I had dealt with every type except Admiralty (disputes about ships and their cargos) and cases involving the International Court at The Hague.[72]

The whole process has become so complex that it is no longer a good choice for a client to take a complex dispute to a reason-

---

72 I was asked to deal with one case where my clients wished to have a trial at the International Court but I had to advise them that they did not qualify as a State (Honestly!)

ably priced High Street solicitor. It is usually in his best interest to choose a big specialist and expensive firm, who in turn, will use the services of a specialist, and expensive barrister.

There are many ideas being floated. For instance, it has been suggested that the public might have direct access to young barristers. In one journal, they were described as 'baby barristers'. I find this tragic but humorous. Can you imagine learning that a doctor who has only been qualified for twelve months should be able to carry out a major operation?

One member of a prominent litigation firm says that for firms to survive, they must 'get big, get niche, or get out'.[73] Another points out that:

> 'Claimants' lawyers fear clients will suffer if novice solicitors are let loose, on cases which they have neither the expertise nor the finance to run. He says that there has been a 'huge increase' in people trying to 'swim upstream' in search of new areas of work. But the effect on clients, many of whom will be vulnerable and unaware of their rights, could lead to 'disasters' along the way.'[74]

There is always a risk inherent in litigation. You cannot know for certain, whether evidence will stand up to cross examination. You do not know what view the judge will take. You do not know whether the legal argument will take an unexpected turn.

I consider that it is not reasonable for a member of the public to find that his only recourse to legal representation is to use an inexperienced advocate. The risk element must increase.

An advocate has to learn his trade but from the point of view of a barrister practicing in the higher courts and possibly with more difficult cases, it has always been helpful for him to have a solicitor there to prepare the case for him and sometimes to

---

73 LSG 29 June 2015
74 LSG 29 June 2105

guide him. I recollect one young barrister who was in just such a situation. He said to me as we sat in court "Please sit between me and the jury. I look so young that they will not believe me. You look older."

The argument about Legal Aid rages on and no less a person than the President of the Supreme Court, Lord Neuberger, was quoted in the Times[75] as stating that:

> 'Rich people can always afford legal advice and representation. Unless you have access to legal advice for poorer people, you have not got the rule of law. We are at risk of denying access to justice and that damages the rule of law.'

Perhaps he went too far when he suggested that, the way in which the legal aid was being restricted was undermining the state, to such a degree, that people might end up by taking the law into their own hands, which is not good for us as individuals or for the country itself. This led to a response from one journalist. He claimed that Legal Aid was spinning out of control. He considered that too many lawyers were being paid too much to bring too many spurious cases. Unsurprisingly, he based his argument on the fact a few barristers, earn as much as £500,000 in a year. The fact is, that many are just earning in the hundreds for representing a man in a defended criminal case. It is said that the average annual earnings of junior barristers is in the region of £42,000.

The journalist claimed that any lawyer who defended the Legal Aid system was exercising naked self-interest. He was claiming that legal aid was available to many people. I consider that he was speaking about people's incomes, without actually understanding how small they were in this context. In fact, if you have a disposable income of more than £733 a month or own property or other assets worth more than £800,000 you will not qualify for

---

75 5th March 2013

Legal Aid in the civil courts. Nor, unless your wealth is greatly in excess of this, will you likely want to take the risk of starting legal proceedings with your own money. If your monthly disposable income is between £315 and £733 a month, on the other hand, the state will pay most of your legal bills. If it is below £315 a month, all costs will be covered. In fact, that leaves a very small band of people who qualify.

I was delighted to see, that soon after that, a lawyer challenged the journalist, pointing out that he was attending a police station to represent a prisoner for a standard fee of £200–£230. This could be for four or five hours work, which is a working rate of £40–£50 an hour. This could be in the middle of the night, he explained.

He pointed out that a court's duty solicitor is paid £55.15 p an hour except if it is Saturday when it is £68 an hour and, if the case is sent to the Crown Court, it could take up to 4 hours.

The lack of fairness to the profession, was even more starkly illustrated by a letter to the Times from some barristers.[76] They had acted in the case where, after a great deal of work, they had managed to prove that the police officers in a case in which they were involved, many years earlier, had been corrupt. Surprise, surprise! They were combative lawyers who persisted until they managed to find the truth. But their point was better illustrated because they pointed out that it was unique in telling how the fee income of barristers had been reduced in the intervening 25 years since they had started. Apparently the lead defending barrister was a junior barrister[77] in 1989. As a junior barrister, he had been paid £100 an hour. Almost 20 years later, a Queens Counsel was being paid £94.50 per hour and a junior, £61 per hour. It is going to be made even worse. In 2014, after the latest costs cuts a QC will be paid just £63.70 per hour and a junior

---

76 4th April 2014

77 In legal talk one refers to a barrister who is not a Queens Counsel as a junior barrister even though he might be quite elderly

just £42.70 per hour. They also pointed out that these are turnover figures for the most difficult cases. There is no holiday pay, no pension entitlement and expenses of about one third of turnover needs to be deducted from these figures.

I submit that this clearly demonstrates that it is going to be unlikely that anyone who needs skilled help to ensure that justice is done is going to find a lawyer who is willing to try to do high quality of work at that price. Again, it is worth a comparison with the medical profession and asking if you told a surgeon that he was going to be paid less than half of what he was paid 20 years ago, for doing the same skilled operation, would he do it on the National Health Service? I doubt it.

The National Health Service is, as the politicians so often remind us, 'free at the point of delivery'. Just imagine what it would be like if you had to pay about £1,000 before actually going through the door of a hospital. That is what is happening with access to our courts. There is now a fee to be paid when anyone starts a civil court case. It is fixed at 5% of the amount claimed if it between £10,000 and £199,000. Claims over that amount will be fixed at £10,000. Apparently the Ministry of Justice believe that the court system should be self funding.[78]

But greater change is planned as I write. The Civil Justice Council has unveiled plans for an internet court service to handle low value civil claims.[79] It was headlined in The Times[80] as 'Judges could rule via Skype in online courts'. It would be restricted to claims under £25,000 and could be extended to suitable family disputes. It is little surprise to read that Richard Susskind is the lead author of the report because he is famous for making inventive proposals for reform. It states that small claims up to £10,000 account for almost 70% of hearings in civil courts in England and Wales. There has also been an enormous increase

---

78 Leeds and Yorkshire Lawyer. Issue 133
79 LSG 16 February 2015
80 16 February 2015

in the fee which must be paid to the courts, before a case is actually lodged. So taking the whole package together, one can see that Joe Public is being forced into a new system, whether he likes or not and whether he feels that he is getting justice. That is said to be progress.

In the days of the general practitioner, in which I practised I dealt with cases that were exciting, sometimes complex, sometimes most satisfying, sometimes evolutionary.

The state of play is changing at such a rate, that I find it difficult to review the many changes. Anything I write today may well be very different by the time anyone reads this.

Lord Justice Jackson looked at the procedures involved in litigation and his famous (or infamous) report suggested considerable changes. It was suggested that it would lead to cheaper and speedier litigation. The profession tried to move away from needless confrontation at each and every stage of the case, as it was being prepared for trial but as I understand it, the changes have not had the desired effect. In fact, they have made matters much more difficult. Once upon a time there was a degree of 'give and take'. If you needed a bit of extra time to complete a particular step, you asked the other side and it was granted. A few days later they might ask you for extra time or some support for getting matters moving in a satisfactory manner. The result of Lord Jackson's report is that people are more aggressive, less cooperative with the result that the litigation process is even more difficult.

A particular problem which has exercised the profession was as a result of the case relating to the Member of Parliament, Andrew Mitchell. He won one case and was granted an order that the other side pay his costs. His solicitors were one day too late in complying with the rules for the provision of some information to the court. The court decided that it was fatal to his claim for costs. This has thrown tremors through the legal profession because there is no give-and-take. It is true to say that as a result of this harsh approach, there are to be changes in the rules. Nevertheless, this is a good example of the unintended consequences which so often follow change.

But I can look back and I will indulge myself by recording some of the varied and interesting cases with which I dealt. This variety of cases, entitles me to describe myself as a common attorney. But I must confess that quite by accident, I became a specialist in a subject which I found to be one of the most interesting and varied. It required an interest in history, as well as law and requiring some skill or experience as an advocate. This is the law relating to public footpaths and associated with that, common land and village greens. Some of the cases that I describe come from that specialism.

But now for some of the ruminations of an old solicitor.

It is always satisfying to make new law. To do so by testing a legal principle in the highest court in the land is a summit of one's legal experience. I had two cases in the House of Lords as it then was. It is now the Supreme Court. The most memorable of them was, when the Ramblers wanted to clarify what was the correct way to interpret evidence about the intention of a landowner NOT to dedicate a public right of way. As there was an adverse ruling some years earlier, which we thought was wrong, we wanted to see if we could overturn it. We lost in the Court of Appeal but took the case to the Lords to clarify or correct the law. It was a fascinating few days. At the time, the judges sat as a Committee of the House. Although the House of Lords Chamber is a colorful and impressive hall, the room in which the judges sat was very small. In other courts they wore wigs and gowns but there the five judges just wore suits. In other courts, the judge or judges are elevated above the advocates and the public. In the Lords they are all almost on a level.

The quality of discussion is astonishing. You have the greatest legal brains in the country there. They listened and discussed for three days and then told us that the judgment would be announced on an unknown date later. You receive a draft of the judgment, a few days before its formal publication so that you can help them avoid any typos and so on. The committee then sat in the big, gilded chamber to formally declare their judgement. We won!![81] It was a champagne moment. But there was a moment that could have put me in prison for contempt of court. Every time that we were about to commence a session of the hearing, the usher, in full evening dress and a large badge of office would remind us to turn off our mobile phones Just before the last session, I was delayed and did not enter the room to hear the reminder. The case finished and we went out into the corridor and at that very moment, my phone rang. It could have been five minutes earlier. Phew!!

The decision in Godmanchester can be summed up as explaining that if a landowner had no intention to allow a public right of way to come into existence because of many years use by the public, he had to show his intention in an open and obvious manner

I was virtually arrested in one court. I had noticed a very interesting statue of a local African explorer in the foyer of the court in Exeter. I thought that I could introduce it into one of my lectures. I took a photograph on my mobile phone and within seconds, an usher 'asked me to accompany him' to the chief clerk. It was an offence to take a photograph in a court building and I had been at risk of being charged with an offence. He accepted my plea in mitigation and I merely received an informal caution.

Then there were the famous Van Heutstraten cases. This story is so well known that I will only dwell on it briefly. Mr. Van Heutstraten owned land at Framfield in East Sussex. He had built an enormous house, which was not quite completed but which, it was said, was not to be become inhabited but was to be his mausoleum. It was said to be the largest house built in England in the Twentieth Century. The land was crossed by a footpath and he had blocked it off at one end with a barbed wire fence, locked high iron gates and some industrial refrigerators. He was on record as saying that Ramblers were the scum of the earth.

---

81 Godmanchester Town Council – v – Secretary of State for the Environment and Cambridgeshire County Council [2007] known as the Godmanchester case.

We asked for a meeting with the highways authority representatives, to convince them to take action against him but they appeared to be unwilling, even afraid. When we attended the meeting, we found that in addition to some senior county officials, there were also some senior police officers present. It seemed that everyone was scared of Mr. van Heutstraten.

We decided that if they wouldn't take action, then we would and we issued the necessary proceedings in the Lewes Magistrates Court. Van Heutstraten would not come to Court. After a few abortive attempts to have the case heard, his solicitor attended simply to tell the court that he could not get instructions and wanted the case adjourning. I submitted that it was just a delaying ploy and the court agreed and decided that it must proceed, whereupon he just walked out of Court. Van Heutstraten was therefore convicted.

His insults about the Ramblers resonated with the public and they were very angry with him and extremely supportive of us. There was a fantastic amount of publicity. There was some risk because it was known that he had a violent background and there was even another case running where it was alleged that he had been involved in a murder (he was convicted but the conviction was later set aside on appeal). Some of my partners were so concerned that they wanted to review the security arrangements in the office. They felt that legal practice was a risky business.

There was another Ramblers' case, where we charged a rather posh landowner with having planted something such as potatoes, across a path. I cannot remember the detail, but part of the defence was something to do with the weather at the time and whether or not my witness could have visited the site on a particular day. I remember that, after a two day case involving some quite heavy cross examination, the Magistrates retired and were out for some time. I was chatting to the defendant and he said to me something such as "You are such an interesting chap. You are the sort of person that I would like to meet in a pub and have a drink with." I took that as a compliment. He was convicted but he never asked me to have a drink!

The Ramblers, at the time, were very keen to bring a number of matters to public attention and this meant that they quite often took people to court and I acted in all of the cases. As I am seeking to tell about the variety of the work of a common attorney, I shall just illustrate how varied life can be. We prosecuted someone in Wales for obstructing a footpath and I went to the court in Conway to present the case. I walked into the court room and everyone was speaking Welsh. I had a moment of panic, but the clerk assured me that a case only proceeded in Welsh, if all the people involved agreed. I did not agree.

Therefore, I was not surprised when I appeared at a public inquiry in Wales and one witness insisted on speaking Welsh and an interpreter came to help. He put a blanket over his head and spoke from behind it. I never understood why he did that, but I was able to have my cross examination translated and the case move on satisfactorily. There are many cases now where an interpreter is required, but it was something of a shock to find the need in Wales, where everyone also spoke English. I suppose that it was a matter of Nationalist pride.

Nun Monkton is a lovely village somewhere near Boroughbridge, with a wonderful 'village green', a maypole and a lovely pub (named after a racehorse, Alice Hawthorn). There was an argument in the village, as to whether it was a 'village green' and therefore better protected or whether it was just common land because there were common rights of grazing over the common. I was acting for the village green faction. We had a three day inquiry, examining the law and facts and I am pleased to say that it was declared to be a village green.

There were two little incidents which related to this case, which are worth recording.

The first is that there was some reference somewhere to an 'entire'. It did not seem to have any significance, but whilst I was cross examining a witness who suddenly turned on me and asked "Do you know what is an entire?" He said it in a rather upper class English way. I had to admit that I was ignorant (I should have just said that I was not there to answer questions). It turns out that it is an un-castrated male horse!

The other thing is that 20 or 30 years later, a solicitor who had become a member of the Yorkshire Dales National Park Authority and with whom I had served for several years suddenly told me that he had been an articled clerk, helping his principal at that Inquiry all those years before. People have long memories.

I was approached by a client who was an ambulance driver, when ambulance drivers throughout the county were banding together to form their own union, The Fellowship of Ambulance Personal. They asked me act for them and I recollect defending an ambulance driver who was alleged to have committed a road traffic offence (speeding or driving without due care) when responding to an emergency. I put forward an emotional defence. It worked and he was acquitted and members of the Fellowship were most impressed. The Government of the day decided that it was uncomfortable about a separate union being created and convened the McArthur Commission to decide whether they could be recognised as a separate union. I found a respected academic and we prepared our case. I read up about trade union history during a holiday. I was most sympathetic to their aspirations, although now I feel that the whole union principle had and has, gone too far. In any event, the outcome was that they had to become part of a larger union and that was the end of an extremely interesting part of my career. Incidentally, when I had a heart attack and was taken to hospital in the middle of the night, the driver was the very person that I had defended many years before.

Is it work for the professional? This is one field where I can give an unqualified answer. Yes it is. It is technical and complex and clearly the work of a professional.

Is it good for Joe Public? Again, I consider that one can give an unqualified answer. No, it is not. Almost every aspect of the changes are against his interest, whether it is the restriction of legal aid, or the constantly changing playing field of who he can consult and on the level of expertise of which he should be assured, or his choice of representative, he is always going to suffer problems and probably not obtain the service of the compensation that he should expect.

Is it good for Common Attorney? Once again I state with certainty, that other than a member of a big specialist firm, he will be the loser.

CHAPTER 9

AN UNCOMMON COMMON ATTORNEY

A MISCELLANY

I started by trying to define or describe the type of solicitor I call the common attorney. I suppose that what I was trying to describe, or explain, was the type of solicitor that I had hoped or intended to be. I also tried to describe what I thought of as a high street solicitor. I wanted to be a common attorney.

In my early days, there were many of those 'all round' practitioners. They were the classic family solicitor. They were good advocates. They were reliable business advisors.

I hoped to be all that but I did not really think that I had the tools. My articles of clerkship had been to a sole practitioner. My principal, did not charge a big premium – it was £500 – I do not know how my parents managed to save up that amount. He dealt almost exclusively with conveyancing, although he was a clever man he had learned how to attract that work. With the aid of an experienced managing clerk, he had a sort of factory line system going. He got the work in through his contacts or old clients. He took each transaction to the exchange of contracts so that it was a done deal and then the managing clerk took over and dealt with the bones of the transaction. I, another articled clerk and the managing clerk, 'perused titles' and drafted deeds of conveyance. My 'oppo' and I, learned from others articled to different firms that there was more to being taught the law than simply routine conveyancing but our principal was not interested. However, every so often, he gave in to our complaints and requests and took on the odd case. We had one accident case and with the help of a barrister, carried it through to a successful conclusion.

We drafted a few, very few, wills. Once, when our principal took on a criminal case, we went with him to court. But the one case that I remember, was the one and only divorce that he took on. I remember it well. It was a very mature couple. She explained that she had been ill. Her husband was out at work and the husband was grateful that the close neighbour and friend, who was a widower, agreed to come in to the house regularly, to see that the wife was fed and watered. These regular visits, of which many were, no doubt, to the bedroom, led to too much familiarity and to her surprise, the result was that at her relatively advanced age she became pregnant. I definitely learned a great deal about human behavior by this one case, although I doubt if I learned much about the law and practice of the divorce courts.

When I opened my practice, I had a promise of some introductions to house buyers, but in my first few months, the promises proved empty and I was willing to accept any work. Other practitioners were willing to send some of the work that they did not want to take on, so I had a few referrals of criminal cases and some relatively simple debt collection cases. Gradually I found that I was attracting such a variety of work that conveyancing was becoming the lesser string to my bow.

I explain this as background and to the fact that I feel as though I have dealt with so many aspects of legal practice, that I can describe myself as an uncommon common attorney. Many solicitors have been more successful and many have become more prosperous, but I doubt if any have had the variety of experiences or the absolute satisfaction that I have had. So please indulge me by reading about some of those experiences. Also, please forgive me if I just pick out some of the incidents of what form part of a larger narrative, to be found in other places.

My first big breakthrough was almost out of the blue and for reasons which are explained 'in another place'[82], I was asked to

---

82 'Tales from an Environmental and Tribal Lawyer' published on Kindle [ebook] and Beecroft Publications [paperback]

represent a Ugandan African Tribe in their claim for the return of their tribal lands which they called 'The Lost Counties'. This was the wonderful tribe known as the Banyoro-Kitara. This was something that (I doubt) any other provincial solicitor has ever experienced. Suddenly, to be asked to act for a sub-state of a Colonial State, for the King (the Omukama) the Prime Minister (Katikiro) and the Parliament (Rukurato) was quite a challenge. What is important, is that it took me down to London, where I was meeting people – particularly lawyers and Ministers of the Crown – of a level that I would have never expected. On one occasion, I suddenly found myself leading the whole delegation and suddenly realised that even as a young and rather raw solicitor, one could 'take on' Queen's Counsel and an Attorney-General as long as you spoke sense. I also learned that I was not indispensable, because when I went off to Uganda and was away for a fortnight, my office still functioned.

My ability to prepare proofs of evidence was to be tested as one of the barristers and I interviewed many witnesses out in the bush. There was one witness, in particular, who I often remember. We were told that there was a Witch Doctor just within the border in one of the Lost Counties occupied by the opposition tribe, the Baganda. He was supposed to have very important evidence.

I met the good doctor, who was my age and knew nothing other than folk tales, which I knew would be of no value to the case. I therefore excused myself and made to leave. The whole village lined up in two rows and I had to walk through them. At the end, there stood the witch doctor and he presented me with two eggs and a pineapple and made some blessing in what I assume was Lunyoro, the language of Bunyoro. I accepted them and made a little speech and went back to the capital town.

The Omukama was giving a cocktail party that night for all the visitors to his Kingdom and I asked him about any significance of the gift. He was most impressed and told me that it was a blessing. He explained that the eggs were for fertility and the pineapple for sweetness. You will have, he told me, two daughters. And lo and behold, I do now have just two daughters.

However, I do not think that many people in Leeds or my clients knew what I was doing or have ever appreciated the importance of it. I doubt if it added a single Client to my practice. It was just the experience and the possible professional, personal and character development.

I often wonder whether or not I boobed terribly and gave up an immense opportunity, The Queen's Counsel on the other side had his Clerk travelling with him and this Clerk was his "tout". He, the Clerk, would go round Colonial Solicitor's offices asking if they had any briefs for the men in his Chambers and sometimes, he told me, they needed to have an English Solicitor. He asked me if I would allow my name to go on the back of some of the briefs. I pointed out that this would make me financially responsible for the fee and therefore I refused to do this. I often wonder if I had agreed, whether I would have built up a Colonial practice, or whether I did the right thing by being cautious. Bearing in mind that we were talking about costs, which in those days would have been thousands of pounds, I have often had my doubts. As lawyers say about many things "so be it" I therefore console myself by saying "so be it."

Another breakthrough which took me into unexplored avenues, at least for a provincial high street solicitor, was that I became the Honorary Solicitor of the Ramblers Association which is a major national body, famous for its many campaigning successes. There have been references already to some of the work that I carried out for them but there was some work that was not the usual activity of a high street solicitor, especially one in the provinces.

The Ramblers were worried that the Water Bill (the proposed legislation to change the regulation of water supply) would have some effect on rambler's access to gathering grounds near reservoirs and this had been a long running concern. The Minister in charge of the bill was Michael Howard (eventually the Leader of the opposition and now Lord Howard). We set up a meeting with him and we took a barrister along. Howard was not at all receptive but the moment that I remember most clearly, was as we made our introductions. Howard immediately said "I remember you, Mr. Pearlman. At the Defence Lands Inquiry you asked the question ..." I cannot remember the question that I had raised at a public inquiry that I had attended many years earlier, but I do remember that I was astonished that he remembered me and the question. Perhaps it was such a bad question!

Not many common attorneys ever have the opportunity of being involved in drafting Acts of Parliament let alone actually drafting a Bill. There are specialist solicitors whose firms are parliamentary agents and they draft bills with or without the aid of counsel. I had dealing with one of these firms on one occasion and was quite amazed by their knowledge of highway law. They acted for British Rail and clearly they had "been through it all before" but their knowledge, both of highway law, as well as parliamentary practice, was most impressive.

My involvement with parliamentary drafting started through what eventually became the Rights of Way Act 1990.

A Conservative MP, Edward Leigh, had come within the first six in the Private Members' Ballot. Although six MPs are deemed to be successful, it is usually acknowledged that only the first three bills will have a reasonable chance of becoming law. Another factor is, that only one MP has to shout "object" and various parliamentary procedures come into play, so there is very little, if any, chance of the bill becoming law.

For reasons which I have never understood, Edward Leigh who was a member for a Lincolnshire rural, and thus agricultural, constituency decided that he wanted to regularise the law relating to ploughing and rights of way and apparently having succeeded in the ballot, simply rang the Ramblers Association and told them that he wanted to co-operate with them and see if such a bill could become law.

The Ramblers approached the Countryside Commission who were interested and the procedure started. We first asked the barrister who has done most of the Ramblers' cases, George Laurence, to draft a bill but this did not please the civil servants because he drew it as a standalone bill, whereas they felt that it ought to be an amendment to the Highways Act. He therefore recommended that he should work jointly with a retired Parliamentary draftsman, called Francis Benyon. Every so often, one meets someone whose sheer intellectual ability is so impressive that you can think of them only as a polymath. In other words, a person with multiple skills and knowledge. I believe that Francis Benyon was one of those.

We had several conferences with him in London or Oxford, where we would tell him what we wanted and which reflected various ideas put to us by other organisations and civil servants. Sometimes these conferences were in the evening and we told him that an answer was required urgently and he would protest that there was no chance that he could deal with the matter on such a tight time scale. I would get to my office in Leeds the next morning and there was a perfect version of a new clause, or a new bill which he had drafted overnight, typed and faxed to me.

Eventually, the bill came before the House of Commons for the Second Reading which is when M.P.s decide whether or not it was acceptable to the House. It gained all party support and I listened with great pleasure, as something in which I had had a hand, was on the way to become legislative law. I say 'something in which I had a hand' but my hand was rather limited. I had just bought a new car and taken delivery one Friday, before I was due at a 9.30am conference in Oxford with Francis Benyon. I had a puncture soon after leaving Leeds and by the time I had all that sorted out, I managed to get to Oxford, just as the conference was ending. This is obviously a moment for true confession. I remember that during the Second Reading debate, the Minister used that lovely phrase about a private member's bill being a fragile vessel, but I am pleased to say that with hardly any amendment, the Bill became law. Our involvement ended after one or two meetings with the various departments who showed an interest in the Bill and it was then taken over by the Government and we were just spectators to this wonderful event. On the other hand, I must say that the mere fact that I was involved, gave me great professional pleasure.

Several years later, at National Council of the Ramblers, David Beskine who was the Campaigns Director of the Ramblers Association and a person to whom I personally, and the Ramblers, owe a great deal, asked to have a chat with me and put forward the idea of drafting our own Right to Roam Bill. This showed incredible foresight on his part and I do not know from where he got this brilliant idea. He was just full of these ideas.

I started to draft a version of the Bill, after considering various parts of the National Parks and Access to the Countryside Act and several of the problems about access to the countryside of which I have practical, legal and theoretical knowledge. I gained a great deal of help and guidance from the panel which David had set up, particularly the two lawyers who served, Richard Harland and John Riddall.

Eventually after many meetings and many discussions, we decided upon the terms of the Bill. There was one major disagreement and that was whether or not we proposed the preparation of maps of open country which we called "the maps approach" or whether or not we had a formula to describe the type of land, so as various areas of land were recognised as being mountain, moor, heath or down a map could eventually be built up. We called this the "words approach".

I preferred the latter, because I argued that if there had to be maps, the process of preparing them would take "forever" and we felt that the cost would be prohibitive. This was a view that was supported by the Ramblers Executive and I eventually prepared a complete Bill. It went through many stages and arguments. I remember that at one stage, we actually sat at a conference specially convened in Stalling Busk, a small village in the Yorkshire Dales where I have a cottage.[83] I suppose that we all played devil's advocate with one or another and we decided that there were at least 60 different changes that were required, to the Bill. Six weeks later we decided not to bother with any of them!

---

83 A Blue Plaque has been erected in the village to commemorate the event.

Again the Ramblers had good fortune in that one of their strongest supporters, Paddy Tipping M.P., was willing to take it up and present it to Parliament, under what is called the Ten Minute Rule. This he did and obtained a favourable response from a great many Labour MPs. But it was clear that it would never reach the Statute Book unless there was a Labour Government.

Then we had an even greater stroke of good fortune in that another of our great supporters Gordon Prentice M.P. drew an early place in the Private Members' Ballot. By that time the Labour Government was in power. He agreed to use the Tipping Bill or a variation of it with some of the refinements that we had decided upon and also some that he himself specifically requested.

In the days before the debate, the Government gave an assurance that they would introduce legislation and therefore though the debate took place, it was in the context of Gordon saying that he was not going to proceed with the Bill. There were two nice things which appear in Hansard which was a permanent record of what went on.

At the beginning of his speech he said:

'My thanks are due also to all the officers of the Ramblers Association, who worked tirelessly to promote my Bill. I shall not single out any individual save one – Jerry Pearlman, who helped me with the complexities of drafting the Bill.'

By that time one of my daughters who was an academic had written fairly extensively about the Right to Roam and had made some critical comments about some of the views expressed by opponents of the concept. Another MP in the debate said:

'The C.L.A.'s claims [that access would be damaging] have been analysed by the University of Hertfordshire … [and] … was …' unmethologicly, unsound and based on inaccurate data … academic speak for a loads of tosh'

It was my daughter, on the staff of the University of Hertfordshire to whom he was referring!

So both of us were being referred to in the same debate in the House of Commons.

The next step was that the Government did honour its promise and introduced the Countryside and Rights of Way Bill. When Government Bill was published, I remember one Government Official saying that my Bill had been wonderful because, instead of having to start with a clean sheet of paper, she could look at my Bill and use it as a framework for her draft.

Throughout the period of the Bill's passage through Parliament, I attended many meetings with Ministers and sat through the Second Reading stage, and several of the Committee stages in the House of Commons and even in the House of Lords.

I suppose that I will be remembered as the Honorary Solicitor of the Ramblers Association but in fact, I have served several other and very different organisations.

My first, rather scruffy office was on the second floor of an old building and on the first floor was an estate agent. He had sold a house to a Mr. Singh and probably was bewildered by the many Sikhs who were involved. I learned that the Sikh community, was buying the house to use as the first Sikh Temple (Gudwara) in Leeds. I remained involved with them for years. I was made the Honorary Solicitor to the Gudwara. Balwant always called me 'My Lord'. They moved into bigger and better premises. The Mr. Singh who had first come to see me was Balwant Singh. They told me that they were to celebrate the 500th anniversary of the birth of their founder Guru Nanak and I became involved in the planning of the event. They had never done anything like this before. It was in Leeds Town Hall with the Lord Mayor who was to open the event. I drafted the invitation letter and even prepared a speakers list with a suggested timetable. One item said 'Lord Mayor (5 minutes). The chairman solemnly announced "I now call upon the Lord Mayor to speak – for 5 minutes."

Mr. S. reminds me that he was one of my first clients in the scruffy office in Albion Street. He reminds me that he was a bus conductor and I acted for him when he bought his first house. He prospered and established a jewellery business. He was a Hindu and became devout and became President of the Hindu Temple in Leeds. He was responsible for a major building project. At his suggestion, I became the Honorary Solicitor of the Hindu Temple. For a while I was Honorary Solicitor to my own synagogue.

Therefore, for several years I was Honorary Solicitor to a Sikh Temple, a Hindu Temple and a Synagogue. At the same time, I was conducting litigation about a dispute between the members of a Mosque. Also, many years ago by way of a misunderstanding we attended a Parochial Church meeting for the parish including the Dales village where I had a cottage, Stalling Busk. We thought it was the Parish Council meeting and it was going to discuss an important proposal for use of our old schoolroom, which is really our village hall. In fact, the only issue of relevance to the village was about the central heating in the church. I intervened to give the benefit of my experience of a case that I had in the office. They invited me to join a sub-committee of the church council, but I thought it prudent to decline!

A MISCELLANY OF EXPERIENCES

Life as an uncommon attorney was not just about dealing with organisations, but it was very much about people and the problems that they brought into the office.

A high street lawyer can find that he is asked by a client to help with many, many different problems. You can sometimes be the family lawyer who understands some of the dynamics of a particular family, Sometimes you are the psychologist or the marriage guidance counsellor. Sometimes you are like a parent warning your client about the error of his ways. Many fit the description that I have used so far, but there are others that fit no category. On the one hand (!) some actual cases or clients have unexpected aspects that stick in the mind. As my mother used to say "Variety is the spice of life." In describing some of the experiences that have stuck in my mind, you will experience the flavour of being a high street lawyer both in and out of court and also in the world of public enquiries, the latter being my more usual venue for my advocacy. For me some of these experiences were exciting, satisfying, amusing, difficult or irritating, but they come to mind instantly and I share them with you.

I had carried out a variety of work for Mr. and Mrs. J. They came in on a new matter. They produced a fairly large pile of ancient documents and told me the following story: There was a tradition in their family that an ancestor had been involved in a Chancery action in the early eighteenth century. Money had been paid into court and the belief was that it was still there. They had heard that any money in court carried interest and by the 1960s they calculated that if £10,000 had been paid into court then it would be worth millions by now. Could I investigate? My study in those days was in my loft and I eventually spread these papers all over the floor and over the course of the next few weeks or months I tried to decipher the documents which were hand written in old script but fortunately, in archaic English and not in either legal French or legal Latin, which two languages were from time to time, the official languages of the courts. The documents were terribly wordy, possibly because the old lawyers are said to have been paid 'by the folio' which was seventy-two words. There was indeed, reference to the payment into court but the pleadings for the case, (that is what most of the documents were), were not complete and there was nothing to show that the money had been paid out. In fact, there was nothing to show whether the case had actually been completed. It was quite possible that it had been won or lost and the matter finished and the money properly disposed of.

However, Mr. and Mrs. J were willing to spend a little money to have Chancery Counsel look at them. I sent the papers to London but counsel felt that there was no way to make sensible investigations and that seemed to be the end of the matter. I think that my clients took the view the 'never venture, never win' but they had ventured and lost and it had been a proper attempt.

That was not quite the end of the story. There was a small postscript. I love second hand book shops and have always been on the lookout for old books on the law, of either highways or commons. I was browsing when I came across a book published by Waterlows in about 1876 which was a list of all money lodged with the great courts of the land in 1875. I realised the significance because I had understood that when the whole court system was overhauled by the Judicature Act 1875, the government took all the 'old money' lodged with the courts and used it to build the Royal Courts of Justice in the Strand. I bought the book for 2/6d but I had forgotten the names of the people mentioned in those old court pleadings. I contacted the clients and we went through the book together but – and I am sorry to have to record – that we never found the name and were not able to pursue the matter any further.

A client [Z] was suing a well known footballer for breach of contract. The case dragged on because the footballer's solicitor was determined not to let it be known that he had entered into several contracts in breach of his exclusive arrangement with Z. As I may have mentioned I had become the Law Society spokesman on Radio Leeds and I used to do a phone in programme for them together with somebody from the City Council and somebody from the Citizens' Advice Bureau. A man rang in and said that he was 'RP' and that he had a problem with a solicitor who wouldn't get on with a case. It was dragging on. What could he do about it? All of a sudden I realised that it was Z and he was really taking the mickey out of me and using his two first names as an alias. I recognised his voice. I knew who it was and I knew that his case was taking a long time. Although he knew the reasons, I was able to answer him in good part.

The 'other side' were clearly trying to avoid disclosing documents and were delaying the case and eventually, I realised that the only way I was going to solve this problem about the missing documents was to go down to Welwyn Garden City and visit the factory of a well known food manufacturer because it was thought that the footballer had been sponsoring their products. I went down there and the man whom I had arranged to see refused to give me any information. I said that I wanted to speak to his superior and was handed over to another person who just got out the file, handed it to me and I was able to find the incriminating document, which I am sure had an enormous effect on the whole case. I then knew what it was like to be a detective who had solved a case. The adrenalin was high and I drove back home as if in a dream.

One of several unexpected experiences kept on cropping up which I looked upon as 'perks'.

One was an occasion involving a chap who was the son of a very important local family, but he always managed to get things wrong, whether about family, property or business proposals. The particular occasion arose from the fact that he had bought a lovely property on Anglesey (we had not acted for him). As far as I can remember, it had no vehicular access, only by foot or boat. He wanted to take his car along his neighbour's property but the neighbour refused to allow him. There was nothing in the deeds but I suggested a site visit. He told me that he had a pilot's licence and he would borrow a plane. He flew me down and we were accompanied by his girlfriend. I do not know if he owned or hired a plane but we left Leeds/ Bradford and he was showing the girl friend how to fly the plane. We used the Holme Moss transmitter as a beacon to be sure that we were on the right route. We landed at the RAF base of Barry on Anglesey where, much later, Prince William was stationed. There was no way that we could establish any extra rights of way, but it was an interesting day.

This was a marvelous case relating to a footpath on the edge of the Dartmoor National Park. A doctor and his wife had bought property, knowing that there was an issue about the footpath which appeared on the definitive map and which crossed the property. The wife did an absolutely fantastic job of searching out every bit of historical information that she could, but the trouble was that the original landowner had not bothered to appeal when the path went on the map. Therefore, on the basis of a legal rule, (the leading case was one of mine) she really did not have a chance.

I remember cross examining for about two and a half hours, going through each part of massive body of evidence and challenging it and showing that it did not necessarily mean what she suggested. When I sat down, I saw her husband was 'staring me out'. I had to keep responding to his stare for quite a while until the Inspector said something to me and I was able to look away! I remember two other perks of this case. They were both about the hotel in which I stayed. It had menhirs inside as part of the walls showing that it was extremely old. I was told that Charles Dickens had stayed there.

I appeared at an inquiry into a major opencast enquiry. I cross examined about the fact the Opencast Executive had not taken into account Section 11 Countryside Act 1968[84] (they produced an assessment the next day!). A leading local environmentalist also appeared and I remember his evidence, namely that he opposed the extinguishment of a public footpath, because he had used it when walking with his wife and they often got down on the ground and made love! I mentioned to the NCB people that I would like to go down a mine and eventually they were able to arrange for all four of us (me, my wife and two daughters) to go down a big mine just outside Pontefract. The children were under age but they were made an exception. It was a great but frightening experience as we crawled through the actual coal face machinery. The noise and coal dust were terrifying. I have never since ceased to admire miners. When we returned to the surface and showered, they gave us strawberries and cream!

P was notorious as a loudmouthed con man who had made and lost fortunes. A neighbouring solicitor and I had never got

---

84 In the exercise of their functions relating to land under any enactment every Minister, government department and public body shall have regard to the desirability of conserving the natural beauty and amenity of the countryside.

on together and I suspect that he had refused to act for P and possibly, as a joke, recommended that he consult me. I will not go into any detail about the business part of the work that I did but there were all sorts of peculiar issues.

One was that some of the evidence required, was held in a Lichtenstein merchant bank. P decided that we had to go out there to see them but first we would visit one of his Swiss lawyers in Zurich. We flew out one Sunday night – travelling business class and according to him, we were to spend the night in a very good hotel in Zurich. As we went through immigration in Zurich, he was arrested. In the second or so, as that happened, he handed to me a roll of money (it was £1000 or thereabouts which was a great deal of money in those days) and he said "Get the (naming a support group in Leeds)."

So I found myself alone in Zurich and knew that I had to do something. I knew the airport and the town so I got on the train into Zurich and went to the hotel and asked for my room which I said was in the name of P. They denied having any booking in that name. I realised that he had probably booked in a false name but they would not accept that I had a booking. There were no vacancies and it was round about midnight! That hotel was good enough to find me another hotel and as soon as I got there, I phoned my wife who contacted the support group which took over and found him a Zurich lawyer.

I contacted the original lawyer who we were to have visited and arranged to see him. He said that P owed him money, but as I was there alone, he would do me the professional courtesy of giving me information. This led to me deciding to go to Lichtenstein, to see if I could get the requisite evidence. However, by that time, one of P's sons had set off for Zurich and we eventually met up at the railway station and caught a train to Lichtenstein.

Then there was one of my best ploys. I suggested that I should go in by myself and only if I had trouble would I call the son to come in. I saw the bankers and they refused to show me any documents because I could not prove that I represented any of the actual clients. I asked them who could authorise them and they said one of the sons! So I went next door to the café, where I had left the son and brought him in and they had to show me the documents, which proved to be vital.

One of my clients had a dispute with a man from Musselborough in Scotland. I either sued him or just wrote to him, with what we called a letter before action. He replied complaining about my clients and then 'it' started. He wrote to me, not once, but twice a day. In those days, there were two postal deliveries and a letter would arrive in each. He had very distinctive handwriting and eventually, I could recognise the envelopes. I just put them in a big box. I learned that he also wrote to my client company and also to each of the directors –also twice a day. I eventually learned that he wrote to the Lord Chancellor, the Prime Minister, the Queen and I think, the Law Society. I do not know if they were honoured twice a day but it could have been so. After more than a year, it just stopped. It must have cost him as much in postage as was the amount of the claim. I am fairly certain that the clients never got their money.

F was a big burly farmer from near the coast. He had sold part of the family farm and had invested in a big deal run by some friends. The idea was that they would buy parts of those new-fangled things – computers – in America, put them together and sell them. In retrospect, I am convinced that many people made fortunes from this business model. In this case, F became suspicious that his partners were ripping him off and he started interfering and went to Los Angeles to find out what they were up to there. He had also raised money from the bank, secured on what remained of the farm. There was some story that he told me that he had taken much of the material and put them in 'a bin', (I found out that a bin in America is a storage unit like, what we now call, self-storage units). There was a dispute about what had happened with the banks in US and one of the possibilities was, that I would have to go to San Francisco and Silicone Valley and interview some witnesses. I did not think that it was necessary, especially at that stage, and Counsel agreed with me. Then the barrister had a slipped disc and we moved to a young man in the same chambers. There was some development and I asked him to advise and he gave written advice which included the recommendation I go and interview the witnesses in San Francisco. I disagreed but I sent the opinion to my client. He phoned me at lunchtime on Easter Sunday and he said that he felt that I should go out there. I disagreed. My wife overheard this and after the phone call she said "I thought that I was married to a sensible man." I asked why and she said "surely you always wanted to go to the Grand Canyon?" I expressed ignorance, saying that I did not know that San Francisco was near the Grand Canyon. So I got out the atlas and as soon as I saw the geography I phoned F back and said that I had reconsidered and now felt that I should go, which we did.

There was one unpleasant incident during the trip. I interviewed one bank official in the presence of the bank's lawyer. I wrote out the proof and he wanted it typing before he would consider signing it. It was given to a secretary and whilst we waited, they talked to one another and ignored me. I had to sit there for over half an hour, feeling like the proverbial lemon. I was livid.

I had just obtained judgment in one of my big Ramblers cases and I was certain that it would be included in the Times Law Reports. A few days later, I was in North Wales, doing an obstruction case in the magistrates' court in Conway. I ordered the Times in my hotel and turned to the Law Reports and saw 'Pearlman Grazin' and thought this will be MY case, but I looked more closely and realised that it was one of my partner's cases (which we had won). I was disappointed and then looked again and suddenly saw my case in the same Law Report! I was overjoyed. Later, we claimed that we were the first provincial law firm to have two cases reported in the Times on the same day! We got that in the local press!

I read once that many successful business people summarise their progress by using the phrase 'Get on; Get Honest: Get honorable.' This adequately describes one client, who gave me the following short autobiography. We were on our way in his chauffer driven Rolls Royce to complete a transaction involving over £1m. He asked the driver to take a route that passed some railway arches, under which, were some wholesalers offering their wares. He explained that he used to visit them on a Friday afternoon and buy goods to sell by retail the next day. He explained that his Bank would only cash the cheque if he paid in sufficient funds on Monday!! It is called 'teaming and loading'! From there, he became a wholesaler himself and then a manufacturer. Now he was so honorable that he was known for his philanthropy.

I remember another journey in a Rolls Royce. My client complained as we drove to a meeting where we hoped to settle a dispute about some vehicle parts. He complained that his new Rolls Royce had a slight noise. I spent the day with the 'other' solicitor, whilst my client went to do more business. As we drove back, I happened to ask whether he could still hear the noise. He said not but when we stopped, he opened the boot and lying there, was a huge commercial gear box swimming in oil. He explained that the weight had stopped the noise.

Bashir Ahmed was the leader of a Muslim faction in Huddersfield. He was involved in a fight and was charged with affray. I instructed Edward Lyons. I remember that Ahmed said, that if we got him off, he would give me a trip to see mosques in Pakistan. The case was heard in Wakefield and lasted quite a few days. I needed someone to sit behind counsel and both my daughters took turns and thoroughly enjoyed themselves. He was acquitted. He forgot his promise. When I had my heart bypass, I was in the high dependency unit where only family are usually allowed in to visit. I was only semi-conscious when I saw at the foot of my bed, the same Bashir Ahmed. He handed me a bunch of flowers and a bottle of Lucozade and said "Get well, Pearlman" and left. I heard later that he had just dropped dead in the street (not the same day!)

A MISCELLANY OF PEOPLE

There were the well known local oddities. Of course there were the regular drunks who had their favourite solicitors who asked for you every time they were found drunk and disorderly and the regular petty thieves. In fact, the magistrates knew them as well as you did. Then there were very sick people who had delusions of one sort or another.

There was the woman who wanted an injunction to stop her neighbours listening through the walls, or, who believed that the police or someone in government had planted microphones in their walls. They were usually paranoid schizophrenics. There was the man who believed that he owned the Crown Jewels and wanted them back. The usual answer that you gave was "I don't deal with that type of work, but I recommend that you go and see Mr. 'X' (depending on who had given you agro recently). "His office is in the next street."

But many people who came to consult me had a really interesting story to tell or had an interesting idea or activity.

There was a well known businessman who was known to think up unusual ways of making a living. He opened a debt collecting agency and instead of the usual way of encouraging a debtor to cough up – strong arm men and the like – he came up with a better idea. He bought a building in a small run down street near the Parish Church in the oldest part of the City. It was, and is, genuinely called High Court. His note paper gave one the definite impression that it was not just a postal address but was the location of the actual High Court. It worked for a while and he built up a good business. His reputation with credit companies grew, but so did the complaints, and the Consumer Credit Office eventually caught up with him. We had to appear before a tribunal in London which made him design his documentation that it no longer gave the wrong impression. Like him or not, like what he dreamt up or not, you have to have a slight degree of admiration for him. After all he was just making a living!

But I had learned early on in my career that you had to be careful who you sent away. My first big case, after opening my own practice came from a dock brief. Before Legal Aid was properly established, if an accused person was arraigned before an Assize court or Quarter Sessions and was not represented, he could look at the backs of the barristers sitting in court and choose one. If the barrister found that it was not just a guilty plea, he could ask for a solicitor to be assigned. This happened one quiet Friday afternoon. I had a small case waiting to be dealt within the Town Hall in Leeds. I was standing outside the court room when the clerk from another court came looking for a solicitor, as requested by a barrister and I was the only one around. I was assigned the case, which developed into a six day fraud trial and was the first in a series of links that lead to me acting for the African tribes and their Kings, that I have already mentioned.

One Thursday, it was Maundy Thursday, I had agreed to meet a potential client (Mr. D) who wanted to stop himself being ordered to remove a provisional common land registration that he had made. I was disappointed to find, that I could not keep the appointment, because I was delayed in court. I asked my assistant to see him. When I got back, the assistant asked me why I had landed him with such a nut case. 'He says that he owns the whole of Thorne near Doncaster – all 49,000 acres and it is because of these old documents', pointing to a cardboard box stuffed to the top with papers. I will only say that it led to a series of cases in public enquiries, magistrates and the High Court and the Court of Appeal[85]. Equally important, it led to me being the first to learn that there was a major source of evidence to prove the existence of public rights of way and some common rights.[86] Once again, I must

---

85 For more detail see 'Tales from an Environmental and Tribal Lawyer' Op. cit

86 Finance (1909–10) Act 1910

disclose, that some of the experiences which followed are written up in 'another place' but I cannot resist mentioning one or two.

I had been dealing with his problem about Thorne Waste for about two months and was beginning to feel that I had no time available for any other work. More to the point, what little time that was usually available, to allow me to go for a walk were becoming less and less. I pinned Mr. D. down to taking me out for a walk over the moor one Saturday afternoon. He was an expert naturalist, as well as being expert at several other disciplines. He really was. He had taught himself to read and translate and transcribe Legal French, which is the language used in many medieval legal and governmental documents. He was a famed amateur etymologist, having identified at least one, otherwise unknown British insect which, he told me, was named after him. And he had a better grasp of history and of the law relating to all those parts of our history which created and preserved common land than any historian or lawyer that I have ever met. He also had a single minded dedication that was simply frightening.

We started our walk over the moor and he explained to me how the peat had been formed and how it was being taken out on a large scale commercial basis, by the Public Company that claimed to own it (it was part of his case that this company did not actually own it but that their title was based upon what he called "fraudulent documents – although I feel fairly confident that he never suggested that the company was a party to the creation of the offending documents). He also showed me the incredible drainage system that Nicholas Vermuyden[87] had created and which still existed over 300 hundred years later. As we walked he started to show me the plants and to my astonishment, showed me a great variety of insect eating plants. I now know that they exist in many areas of the country, especially the wet lands, but the first knowledge is always the most exciting discovery.

---

87 He was a Dutchman famous because he built the polders which enabled the Dutch to reclaim much land.

After about half an hour, I was already very impressed and I suggested to D. that what I had seen so far, would be of such interest to young people that he ought to bring parties out on to the moor and show them what he was showing me. He replied that it was not practical because, as he put it, the whole area was too dangerous. I assumed that he meant that the water in the drainage channels and canals was so deep that it was the source of the danger but he said "No, it's because of the snakes". He went on to explain that the moor was home to innumerable adders, which could be dangerous if disturbed. Nothing of that nature had occurred to me and I thought that he was exaggerating and so I said "If you see a snake then show it to me", thinking that I would call his bluff. So about half an hour later, when he said "Did you see that snake?" pointing in to the undergrowth, and as I had seen nothing, I scoffed at him. An hour later he said "Look there's another snake" and once again I looked and saw nothing and again, I scoffed.

This time he had obviously decided to test my bravery. He broke off a twig from a nearby bush, waded into the undergrowth and poked around and suddenly drew out the twig with an adder dangling on the end. He then said "Have you ever seen an adder's fang?" and to demonstrate, pushed his other hand into a pocket and withdrew it, now clothed in a thick leather glove. He drew the adder and the glove towards one another and suddenly the adder's head struck towards the glove, I quickly saw its fang strike the glove, and there on the glove was a small pool of liquid which D. assured me, was its venom. He then released the snake; it must have felt the greater sense of relief than even me. After I had expressed my astonishment D. told me that he sometimes accepted commissions to collect snake venom for research purposes and that it was a dangerous occupation. He told me that on one occasion, when in the most remote part of the moor, he had been bitten and he knew that he did not have enough time to get medical help. As he spoke, he drew out of a sheath on his belt, a large bladed knife and demonstrated that he had cut two large incisions on the part of the finger where he had been bitten. He showed me how he had sucked out the poison and then spat it out. I then saw what I had never noticed before. He had a large cross shaped scar on the side of one finger. I later found that the large bladed knife, which apparently was always on his belt, was not his only weapon. I eventually found, that he always carried a revolver in a shoulder holster. But that is another story!

The other story that I shall tell about him, is that early in our association, he told me that although he was tee-total, he was an expert wine maker and that some of his wines were a good remedy for colds and coughs. My late father often suffered from chest troubles and became addicted to D's medicine, but I never found out if it was the medicinal or the intoxicating powers, that he found best. D. also told me that he had discovered a method of producing spirits, which was not distillation and therefore, not contrary to the Licensing Act. He gave me a bottle with a label which read 'D's Thorne Moor Witch Piss. For honest solicitors and true conservationists. Dare you try some?' One night, he phoned me at home and my then 6 year old daughter answered the phone. He gave his name and asked to speak to me. She yelled out to me in a loud voice, which he clearly heard "Daddy, there's Mr. Witch-Piss on the telephone for you!" He took it in good part!

Just a little post script to that. He also gave a bottle to the Queen's Counsel, who represented him at the first of his High Court cases, in which I was involved, Mr. John Balcombe Q.C., later Lord Justice Balcombe. He told me years later, that he took the bottle home and told his wife the story. She recommended that he pour it down the kitchen sink. He did so and it burned the silver off the bottom of the sink.

I am not a betting man (that reminds me of another story) but I will wager, that there are few common attorneys who can claim they have had a more varied and exciting career than me.

CHAPTER 10

THE DYING EMBERS BUT A SPARK OF HOPE?

Note my use of a question mark!

When I started writing, my aim was to make a comparison between then and now. 'Then' was when I opened my own practice in the late 1950s. 'Now' is how I see it as I write.

'Then' all I have to do was put my plate up. I informed the Law Society and then applied to have my name placed on certain legal aid lists. I also applied to a number of building societies to ask them to put me on their panel. I have already dealt with that earlier. It is very different now. The first, is that now a solicitor cannot start his own practice, until he had been qualified for at least three years. Now, I gather that there are hardly any sole practitioners. Most of them are in partnerships, whether of just two people or many more.

Some of the statistics that I have noted are these (although it is difficult to find all the figures in a form which lends itself to making a comprehensive comparison):

- In 1951 there were 17,396 solicitors on the Roll. In 2012 there were 160,394
- The overall number of firms, in 2012 stood at 10,976, fractionally more than *th*ree years later but the figures are changing dramatically. The Annual Statistics Report 2014 discloses that it was down to 9807 in 2013 and 9542 in 2014.
- The biggest increases are in the number of incorporated companies which had almost doubled to 2980 and by 2014 was 3323.
- The number of LLP's (Limited Liability Partnerships) has also expanded, from 1101 in October 2009 to 1541 by December 2012 and to 2667 by 2014.

- The Gazette commented[88] that the number of law firms has dipped to its lowest level for many years, which suggest that long predicted consolidation has become begun in earnest.
- Traditional partnerships continue to decline down by 86, month on month, to 2681 and more than 1000 in August 2009, when the Solicitor's Regulation Authority began keeping records. The number in 2014 was 6461

Traditionally, solicitors were either sole practitioners or were in partnership with unlimited liability. Partnership was important. The ideal partnership being one which had a reasonable spread of 'finders, minders and grinders' without one partner considering that he was under appreciated and considering himself to be 'the milk cow of the practice'. It was also said that an ideal partnership, was one which may have had its partnership agreement in the safe but they had never had cause to take it out.

Once we were willing to tell Joe Public that we were willing to back our reliability, by acknowledging that, subject to indemnity insurance, we took personal responsibility for our advice and our actions. On the other hand, we had some protection. It was not real protection, but there was a belief that one lawyer would not sue another. It was not true then and not true now. I was once told that 'Abuse of a lawyer is remembered in costs.'

The introduction of Limited Liability Companies (LLPs) has changed that. We can limit our liability by the creation of such a vehicle. I wonder if Joe asks himself 'what is the maximum that this common attorney is good for?' But the concept of limited liability, combined with that of the Alternative Business Structure has taken the solicitor's branch of the profession, down a very deep step, almost as though it has slipped down a cliff. A firm of solicitors is reported to be taking itself to the stock exchange.[89]

---

88 November 2013
89 Sunday Times 07.07.15

On that basis, any Tom, Dick or Harry can take the profit (if there is any) from giving legal advice. And the liability of the firm to its clients, is limited. I shed a tear when I read the news.

As I drew upon my memory, I was constantly reading in the newspapers and particularly, the 'journal of gloom' and doom known as, the Law Society's Gazette (LSG), of the many changes that were planned or were taking place. I developed a deep sense of foreboding. The profession as it is at the moment of writing, is so different from what it was in my 'old days' that it is hardly recognisable. I started to make notes of the changes and what follows is a selection of the comments and statistics which have appeared. Mainly from the Gazette. The situation is very fluid and will change as soon as I have completed my record and the statistics will be very different. We will know better, whether some of the pessimists are correct, but I am convinced that much of their pessimism will prove to be well placed. So consider some of the information and comment that I have culled.

The changes are likely to go to the very root of the profession and to such a degree that the very structure of the world that we solicitors knew will disappear. There is talk of there being a review of the future regulation of the profession.[90] There could be 'deregulation' which I take to be weakening the foundations. I see the possibility of a free for all in the provision of legal services. So will that lead to a lowering of standards? The President of my own Local Law Society in Leeds, is reported as warning that the rise of providers who can call themselves lawyers but have little or no qualification, is threatening the future of the legal profession.[91]

One threat is the emergence of a number of, what I can only describe as, conveyancing factories. Reputable firms have set these up to offer a fixed service at a fixed price, but one size does not fit all. They are to be congratulated for finding a well managed

---

90 LSG 23 November 2015.
91 Colin Gilbert. Leeds and Yorkshire Lawyer. November 2015

procedure, which employs every IT and procedural service, to cut the work to the bone but the client does not have the feeling of confidence, because he never sees a face and never has a shoulder to cry on, when there is a delay or a problem. There are also the Tesco type proposals, where a big business organisation uses the concept of an Alternative Business Structure, which is set up by a non-lawyer but employing or in partnership with, a lawyer. They probably hope to take the cream off the milk. There is now also a proposal that those who now have the qualification of a Legal Executive (the old managing clerk as mentioned earlier) should be able to set up shop and offer conveyancing services equivalent to Licensed Conveyancers. [92]As I see it, it is just another nail in the coffin, of the high street solicitor.

There have been attempts by some firms, to venture into estate agency and to offer a complete property service. There are some, but only a few, who have continued along this route and they are mainly in rural areas. Apparently, it has not proved to be the panacea that some expected.

The approval in 2012 by the Office of Fair Trading of a Will Writers Code of Practice is yet another tack [a small nail] in the coffin.

My fear is supported by an item in the Law Society Gazette[93] at the time of writing which reports that the Solicitors Regulation Authority (SRA) was supervising more than fifty firms at risk of financial collapse. That would have been unheard of, a generation ago. Recently, there have been three high profile insolvencies which have hit the headlines. I am aware of one old established firm, in my own town, which has had an insolvency administration. The Gazette later reported [94]that 30 leading firms were in serious financial trouble. It reported that 20% of the 160 firms which were in 'intensive engagement' talks about

---

92 LSG 2 December 2010.
93 Law Society Gazette 27 May 2013
94 17 June 2013

their finances rank amongst the top 200 firms. Eight of the 200 were said to be at immediate risk of collapse. The Financial Times claimed that in July 2013, between 3000 and 4000 of the 11000 UK law firms will disappear over the then forthcoming three to five years, as they face a 'perfect storm'. The Times[95] reported that the regulator had said that about 50 law firms in England and Wales were in 'intensive care', the most serious level of difficulty. It went on to say, that observers speculate that the SRA has significant concerns over many more, and by its own acknowledgment, it had written to some 2000 'high impact' firms, including the top 200, asking for financial details.

A clue as to how the legal scene could evolve, was shown in comments in the Gazette.[96] Smaller practices will disappear because of 'a consolidation process, driven by new investors in the sector' in other words, big fish are eating up the minnows. AIM listed companies buy solicitors firms, private equity firms invest in (and thereby, probably eventually run) solicitors firms and some firms buy out others such as the purchase of an English firm, by an Australian one. One can imagine the high street being lined by the legal supermarkets, all with the same shop front, logo and uniforms! Is that the end of such a proud profession?

A most remarkable survey has been carried out by the accountants, Baker Tilley.[97] Nothing that I have read has depressed me more. Their research, showed that at the time of their survey, the Solicitors Regulation Authority had issued 144 Alternative Business Structure (ABS) licences and there were then more than one hundred in the pipeline. I mentioned Eddie Stobbart and Betfair earlier, but Baker Tilley listed insurance companies, estate agents and even the AA, as participants. They quote one solicitor who is involved, who says:

---

95 12 September 2013
96 Law Society Gazette 1 March 2012
97 Legal Innovation 2013. New developments in an old profession'. www.bakertilley.co.uk

'The big game changer is the power of technology to pull back the curtain of mystique. We largely gave up paying scribes to read and write for us centuries ago and there is now no longer any reason why we need to pay someone to tell us what the law says and how it can be applied. Many lawyers still cling to the view that their websites shouldn't give away the 'Crown Jewels' – that is, they should tempt you into the shop but not tell you anything that will make this unnecessary. This is the view that will soon mean no one will even bother to look in their window'.

Whilst I think that I have some understanding of the reasons, which have made the government deal so harshly with legal aid, I consider that it is a disaster. Perhaps the first reason, is that the government is committed to preserving the National Health Service. Just imagine, if the National Health Service was changed, so that there could be no free consultation with the doctor, because you only had a bad chest and no free medication to alleviate the symptoms

I have always considered that the Legal Aid System could easily and properly be called the National *Law* Service. If the government decided to withdraw health care and rearrange its provision, in the same way as it has been dealing with legal aid, I suggest that there would be riots on the streets. Lawyers are easy game and as I mentioned earlier, the constant thought is 'Let's kill all the lawyers' so it is the law, lawyers and the legal system, which may be seen by governments as a good, soft target.

Another reason for the financial problems of some firms, is the restrictions on legal aid. Indeed the SRA commented that the cuts have made legal aid work economically unviable, for many practices. One of the themes, which I have had to use in several places, is the effect that the restrictive changes in the availability of legal aids are having, on the common attorney and on Joe Public. I condemn it as a political and social scandal and a disgrace and a disaster.

The position with criminal work, is as bad and probably worse, because the actual freedom of the citizen is at risk. As I have mentioned, the amount of criminal cases has surprisingly reduced, largely because the police try to have the perpetrator of a lesser (or not quite so less) crime, accept a caution.

At least the concept of Price Competitive Tendering (for Legal Aid Funding) is being rethought by the government. One way of looking at the package on offer, is rather like the despotic state, where you can only have a government appointed lawyer who has other thoughts on his mind than just looking after his client.

A retired High Court judge Sir Henry Brook is reported[98] as condemning the government's current intention to severely restrict legal aid and he says that the court process is a 'valuable safety valve' for people who think that they have been wronged and he warned.

> 'If you deny access to the courts, you are bottling up resentment that will spill over elsewhere. There will be disorder or simply distrust of politicians, the police and the government. This is a very serious contemporary problem'.

In other words, he fears anarchy. I see what he means and I can only hope that he is wrong.

And a regular writer in the Gazette, Roger Smith, formerly the director of Justice, wrote[99] that it broke his heart, to see what was the best access to justice provision in the world, being broken up by the legal aid changes. He considered that nothing could replace the national network of face-to-face legal services, using private and not-for-profit providers, that we had before the government came into office.'

There is a possibility that the Government has (once again!) got it wrong. A correspondent in The Times[100] suggested that the proposals would be condemned by the courts, as being contrary to EU

---

98 Law Society Gazette 29 July 2013
99 LSG 10 February 2014
100 Robert Morfee 13 March 2013

law. He points to Article 47 of the Treaty of Lisbon, which guarantees legal aid to all those, who lack sufficient resources, to obtain legal help and also EU Directive 2002/28/EC which deals with access to civil justice. I hope that he is right, but I hold my breath.

There could be one very surprising aspect of all this. One of our most senior judges, was reported in The Times[101] as suggesting that cuts to legal aid, will lead to more 'public schoolboys' and fewer talented women reaching the pinnacle of the legal profession. She explained, that as younger advocates at the criminal bar, earn less than £20,000 during the first few years as a barrister, they will not be able to enter the profession.

We hear about the doctor in the accident and emergency unit who is working so long and so hard that he is a danger to the patient. It has been reported that three quarters of lawyers are more stressed now, than they were five years ago. Half of those questioned, said that they occasionally felt at breaking point. There is even an organisation called Law Care[102] It is summed up by the statement of the Law Society, Chief Executive:

> 'There is fiercer competition in the legal market than ever before, and many of the assumptions that have underpinned the nature and status of practicing as a lawyer are being challenged in this difficult environment. Tough economic conditions combined with the legal services liberalisation, changes to legal aid funding and the civil costs regime are having a major impact on the business models of many firms'.[103]

I do not like to be pleased about someone else's problems, but I noted, with some quiet satisfaction, that it was reported that the Co-operative Legal Services had made a loss for the first half

---

101 Baroness Hale 19 April 2014
102 Law Society Gazette 22 Aril 2013
103 LSG 22 April 2013

year of 2013, although they intended to 'continue with ... plans to develop this growing business.'[104]

Even if the competitors are not putting lawyers out of business, the insurance companies may well do so. A major problem is for firms, often the small but sometimes large, to find professional indemnity insurance.

In October 2013, the Gazette reported, that the known number of law firms facing closure, after failing to secure professional indemnity insurance, had jumped to 275. I often wonder how the small practitioner can avoid being truly negligent. He is under enormous pressure in terms of fee income, competition and an increasingly complex legal environment. It is no surprise to me to learn [105] that claims against solicitors were up by 196% in 2014 compared with 2013.

Yet another threat, is not a surprise and was expected by many solicitors. Barristers are not happy. The Criminal Bar Association has launched a campaign aimed at 'levelling the playing field' between barristers and solicitor-advocates, who they allege, enjoy an unfair competitive position. Their chairman claimed that:

> 'junior barristers were being denied access to the cases that would enable them to become tomorrow's QCs and judges, because of the damaging imbalance in practicing rules.'[106]

The bar is starting to offer direct access for the public, As Amanda de Winter, the founder of 'Barrister and Co.' which offers direct access to a barrister explained[107]:

> 'The younger Bar that is struggling to get work, will be more open to looking at new ways to do business. Cer-

---

104 LSG 2 September 2013
105 LSG 6 July 2015
106 LSG 17 November 2014
107 Leeds and Yorkshire Lawyer Magazine Issue 127

tainly, if any junior members are struggling to get tenancy at the moment, because things are tough, they can give us a call.'

And barrister-led businesses are set to go into competition with solicitors firms, the Bar's Standards Board, revealing that it had authorised 15 regulated entities. There have been 90 expressions of interest in the development.[108] They are even offering advice through 'virtual chambers' by video links. This, it is claimed, will allow clients to talk to barristers through a window on the chambers website, with the intention that they will instruct the barrister directly.[109]

Nigel Lavender Q.C. when chairman of the Bar Council complained[110] that circuit judges were concerned that 'relatively inexperienced solicitor-advocates were being fielded by their firms (for what were presumed to be commercial reasons) in cases beyond their capability.' However, speaking about the Bar he did say:

"We have survived Oliver Cromwell, and we have survived Judge Jeffreys[111], 'and I believe that we will survive anything that this or any other government throws at us."

Of course, the bar and thus the judges, who mainly come from the ranks of barristers do not really like the solicitor's branch, but that is another obsession of mine.

Roger Smith in the Gazette[112] thinks:

'A lot of solicitors' routine work will disappear. So will lots of routine jobs. We will be fewer. But the essence of

---

108 LSG 13 April 2015
109 LSG 20 July 2015
110 LSG 17 November 2014
111 Known as the Hanging Judge
112 11 January 2016

the lawyer as ethical, informed, practical and successful problem-solver should remain'

But I question whether the present generation of clients want that. They just wants results and it wants them quickly and cheaply and I do not think that we can make a profession out of that.

But how will we compete with Eddie Stobbart and his ilk? I see that there will only be chains of high street solicitors, rather like the Tescos and Waitroses of the High Street. I see no other way to keep alive unless we band together. There will be the odd firm or individual, who stays outside the rat race but he will have to have little expectation of a high income; he may be a specialist in such a narrow field, that others will refer their cases to him; he may be consumed by a desire to do something special, but he will be in the minority.

I mentioned the demise of many pubs. Many pubs that have survived have diversified or developed into gastro pubs or specialise in, say, many varieties of draft beer. Those that survive have had to change their ways. Look at the number of garages which incorporate a small supermarket or so called convenience store, quite a few of which, now sell alcohol. We might have to learn lessons from those that have survived and copy their model. Perhaps we must increase our product range. Why not be a one stop shop for law, tax, accounts and even a post office. It may demean the profession but it could keep it from burning.

In other words, we will not be dead but we will be transfigured. I will watch, perhaps from afar!

As the President of the Law Society wrote[113] in the year in which we were commemorating the 800th anniversary of Magna Carta and after reviewing many of the changes introduced in recent years, many of which I have already mentioned, we have to be concerned that the Human Rights Act faces destruction.

---

113 LSG 2 March 2015

'Human Rights should never be used as a political tool. Any changes should broaden guarantees of rights rather than seek to limit them – especially in a year when we are celebrating the birth of our fundamental freedoms. It is surely what the remembrance of Runnymede deserves.'

I started to record my recollections and thoughts before I read about a stimulating book, by a well known lawyer and IT expert, Richard Susskind called 'The End of Lawyers? Rethinking the Nature of Legal Service'[114] I differ from him in some respects, but compared with him, mine are the musings of an amateur. I noted that he also used a question mark in his title. He can speak with much more authority than me, but as I read his views there may be massive changes in the way in which lawyers do their business but there is still some scope for the Common Attorney – or at least I hope so. So much of the work which was the preserve of the lawyer is now being whittled away by those who think that it is a carriage on a gravy train. There may not be enough left to enable a lawyer who wishes to help the ordinary man walking down the high street (the so-called man on the Clapham Omnibus) and to be able to earn enough to run his office and also have enough left to buy his food. And I am not joking, as I will demonstrate. Knowing that, despite the commitment of some young person, to help his fellows he may see the prospect of having some reasonable return for his investment in his legal studies as being so low that he may think twice about entering the profession.

Susskind tells us that Lord Neuberger takes the view that:

'civil justice and the preservation of civil society (through enforceable contracts and property rights, for example) are the foundations upon which nation states are built and so should have a first call on public funding.'

---

114 Oxford University Press. 2008

I am sure that this statement has a considerable element of truth but if so, it seems as though the present government policies with regard to public funding, are completely undermining the foundations upon which our state is built.

Even though Richard Susskind sees an office run or equipped much as my practice was, or as it developed, he takes it just a step forward. The type of law service which he envisages, includes technological developments such as video conferencing and which therefore can be improved and streamlined. I have a genuine belief in the way that Susskind tells of the need for more use of modern technology, leading to such techniques as automated document assembly, farming out legal research to a specialist and so on. He suggests a new concept that he calls a 'legal triage' rather like the identification of the injury in an accident and emergency clinic and in so far as, he may be referring to the common attorney, he considers that they must be offering pro bono work.

We all like to think that we are helping ... Whether helping the widow (the widow's mite) or the big business man and many of us have been offering a degree of help on a pro bono basis but we are recommended that we adopt this as an obligation. A former President of the Law Society (who apparently held the post of the attorney-general's pro bono envoy – whatever that is) suggests that we should aim to devote a minimum number of hours per year to pro bono work.[115] Although I would not discourage such an aim, I question whether any other profession is subject to such a recommendation. Can you imagine an accountant or an estate agent having a policy of carrying out pro bono work? I am sure that some do, but my guess would be that you would have to go a long way to find one.

On reading the concept of a triage, it seemed to be that he was describing my own high street office, when I first founded my own legal firm or practice as we called them, and much of what he also envisaged was introduced into my practice, as it devel-

---

115 LSG 29 October 2015

oped and innovation was applied by me and my partners, to the way in which we worked. Indeed, I look upon my office then, as a sort of triage. I directed clients to the member of my firm, most suited to deal with their problem that I identified. Each of us developed a particular interest or knowledge or skill; we often directed clients to the Marriage Guidance Council (now Relate) or to a barrister. We offered some advice on a pro bono basis and in particular, it was common practice to offer the first hour or half hour on a pro bono basis. We introduced the computer at a fairly early stage (who would now think of an office without a computer?). We had standard documents and standard procedures to guide us. We used our trainee solicitors to research the law. I consider that the common attorney – the high street solicitor, offered and had for years, offered the man on the Clapham Omnibus the very type of service that Susskind envisages. But there is a problem – the elephant in the room – and that problem, is money – the 'mite' that I mentioned much earlier.

Susskind, in a later book[116] seems to think that there will only be a rump of what he calls 'craftspeople' or empathisers. I see the force in what he says. What the robot will do for industry, the computer will do for the common attorney. Willingly, but regrettably, I adopt the concept that there will only be a 'rump' left.

So what are the strands that I have noticed in the recent past and how do I fear that they could end up?

The public often see the solicitor as a portly, well fed and quite rich gentleman, who has an ability to twist words. I have noted that many politicians, who are the loudest critics of the legal profession are the first to turn to them, when they have a problem and are often the first to sue, for instance, for defamation. But most of them, see him primarily as an expensive provider. Susskind is not alone in advocating a still greater use of IT. The legal profession as a whole, is recognising how important it is. But

---

[116] The future of the Professions by Richard Susskind and Daniel Susskind. 2015

it costs money both in terms of hardware and software. Someone has to pay for it. The mere fact that a text book can be consulted electronically, does not mean that it is materially cheaper.

The more pro bono work that we do, the more we must earn, to keep the office running. We still have to pay the rent (at high street levels) and staff, even if we dispense with the need for secretaries with the use of speech recognition programmes. There must be someone to greet the client at the door and answer the telephone. There must be someone to keep the accounts in order, in this extremely regulated world and we must have enough at the end of the week to have enough left to feed us. Who wants to consult a lawyer who is not aware and knowledgeable about the world and to understand the bases of money, investment, human relations, one who has developed through study and experience a view of the world so that he is a man of the world, the family solicitor, the chap that you can rely upon?

Instead, we find a profession trying to find a way which could help alleviate the effect of all the changes which are happening, threatened or follow from such ideas or planned or envisaged by such as Susskind. There are those who are questioning whether they can even offer that service which for generations has been the bed rock – some say the milk cow – of the high street solicitor, namely conveyancing. Whilst aspects of the procedure have been simplified, there are a whole series of problems for each firm, each one of which, requires a clear financial input or the time involved is costly in terms, say, of overheads and wages. Professional Indemnity Insurance premiums have soared; even the cost of the annual practicing certificate has increased to £1000, the regulatory requirements such as money laundering requirements are difficult and the requirements of the code of conduct including a lengthy client engagement letter, add to the difficulty of finding enough time to deal with actual problems that a client brings. I heard of a City solicitor claiming that it cost him or the client £2,500 in just opening all the files and documents and going through the checks for a new client, before he starts to actually do any work for the client.

There are certain parts of legal practice, where the flame burns brightly but it is not the usual place for the common attorney. This is the age of the specialist whether it is as a commercial lawyer, dealing with companies or commercial property. There are so many specialist fields, such as medical negligence, planning, employment, insolvency, human rights, patents, building disputes, it goes on and on. I was told of a client who arranged to meet his chosen lawyer in a large firm of solicitors. He had given advanced warning that he was coming in to discuss the purchase of a fairly large manufacturing company. When he arrived, he found a room already occupied by five solicitors and it was explained to him that one was the company specialist, another the property specialist, there was the employment lawyer and another, the patent lawyer and the one who held it all together. He was told that no one solicitor in the firm was qualified to cope with all the problems which *might* be relevant. No doubt, everything was perfectly dealt with, but I am sure that it will have cost him.

I knew that many other firms had their own standard documents and as soon as word processors became the norm, this practice grew. We had our own set of standard documents such as, contracts of various types, employment documents, leases and many, many others. However, the fact that they do not have to be typed every time, means that there is a temptation to add in every possible clause and one's standard document just grows and grows. There is another side to the coin. If you are not cautious, you can just print out the standard document and leave in some clauses which are probably wrong and if you just rely on the previous chap who used it, you might leave out something important.

We have to be kept up to date as the law and practice change. I had an embarrassing moment. I had submitted my standard form of lease to a leasehold specialist, who was on the other side. We met to discuss amendments. My lease had a standard provision that any money overdue would carry interest at, say, 'two per cent over Lloyds Bank base rate for the time being'. The chap suggested that it should refer to Libor instead of Lloyds Bank base rate. I did not even know what 'Libor' was so I disagreed. He said that it was now the normal standard reference. What could I say? I still refused but I looked it up the moment that he left! I think that was the moment when I decided on the basis of 'discretion is the best part of valour' that I should cease trying to deal with matters, with which I was no longer sufficiently knowledgeable, qualified or up to date. I am certain that it was a good decision for me and also a good decision for my clients.

But for the rest of us, there is a spark of hope, as reported by Roger Smith[117] when commenting on a human rights lawyer investigating the murder of Baha Mousa in Basra:

> '... a dedicated solicitor actually willing to mortgage his own house as his clients fought for legal aid eligibility'

If there is a spark, then hopefully the profession will blow on the embers and perhaps a flame will emerge which will grow into a real fire and the profession will be saved and the public will continue to receive the help and support which they need.

There are other competing views. The Legal Services Consumer Panel amazingly predicted that access to justice, will be enhanced if consumers of legal services handle more of their own legal affairs.[118] They envisaged self-layering (whatever that means) as commonplace, as consumers sought alternatives to lawyers, or use them in different ways and thought that consumers would be 'empowered by strengthened rights'. But to my surprise, knowing how politicians usually hate lawyers, a Labour M.P. albeit a solicitor, said:

> "Lawyers have gone through training, shelled out for professional indemnity insurance and are experts" he said 'Yet somebody can toddle along, say they are a McKenzie friend and start undermining and undercutting solicitor'

---

117 LSG 8 July 2013
118 LSG 24 November 2014

I come to a conclusion which is much the same as where I started. There are two sides of the coin. I am the two handed lawyer. Some things are good for the common attorney and some things are now bad. Some things are better for Joe Public and some are worse.

First of all, I consider that the law and the profession are more open. Instead of a training contract (the replacement term for articles of clerkship) one can become a solicitor by showing that you have gained experience 'by equivalent means' and the first paralegal has become a solicitor after four and a half years' experience[119]. Whether it be the Internet generally or Wikipedia in particular, more people can check on the net to find out what their interpretation of the law is and they can then discuss that with their lawyer.

Some of the advocacy skills and the commercial approach to the businessman's problems are now so complex, that there will always be a place for commercial lawyers, but they are unlikely to fit the profile of a common attorney that I am seeking to illustrate.

I consider that information technology and the use of computers is of great value, both to Joe Public and the lawyer.

I consider that competitive pricing is beneficial to Joe Public, but it is sometimes at the cost of the lawyer not making a reasonable, adequate or proper income, from the work that he does. On the other hand, in the commercial age, it is reasonable that Joe Public should get the best bargain that he can.

I think that the worst issue of all, is the withdrawal of legal aid and the unfairness and possibly injustice that this can bring about. This is very bad for Joe Public. Whether it is about his divorce, his children, or the fact that he has been prosecuted, the fact that he has been insulted, would like to make a will but wants make sure that it is right or have the satisfaction that his estate will be properly administered. These are all things that I think, are bad for Joe Public and they are also bad for the common attorney.

---

119 LSG 20 April 2015

The Gazette reported[120]

> 'Morale is at rock bottom amongst criminal practitioners, as they await the outcome (of the Society's legal challenge to the legal aid crime duty tender process) but:
> 'However, while practitioners warn of a 'brain drain 'of talented solicitors, there are still young, passionately committed lawyers determined to make a go of it. Recently qualified solicitor Sarah Magill says: 'For me it is crime or nothing. There is no money in it but I am so happy in my job."

Even the President of the Law Society says[121] that the cuts to criminal legal aid could leave parts of the country:

> 'where there's simply no one left to provide representation to defendants up against the weight of the state. A fundamental tenet of the justice system is that people have access to legal advice and to a lawyer of their choice ... if that goes, there would be a real danger to the justice system and its international reputation.'

I have tried to blow on the embers and ensure that the spark develops into a flame and become a warm fire, but I feel that it is increasingly difficult. Every time I have decided that enough is enough and I should stop completing this litany of despair, I read or hear, about yet another proposed change and another dampener. A partial list compiled by a recent contributor to the Gazette contained Legal aid, small claims court fees and online dispute resolution; costs; training; regulation; liberalisation and then he said that he could go on.[122] I have not even

---

120 26 January 2015
121 The Times 23 July 2015
122 LSG 1 February 2106

included some of his chosen concerns. A headline in the Times forecast that 'Women [are] set to dominate legal landscape in 2020'[123] but then adds:

> 'The high street or village solicitor – typically with brass plaque on the door stating 'commissioner for oaths' who handles everything from divorce to probate is all but extinct. The traditional face of the solicitors' profession is changing so fast that in five years it will be almost unrecognisable from how it looked a generation ago.'

And then commenting upon a new report by the Law Society called 'The Future of Legal services' says that 'Globalisation will write off local solicitor'.[124]

To add to the sense of gloom, the Law Society Chief Executive has written an article for the Gazette[125] under the title 'The end of our profession?' It is difficult to know whether she sees the end or a sort of reincarnation. It is worth pondering upon what she says. She recognises:

> 'Paradoxically, people who are the most qualified and trained (solicitors) are the most regulated, and people who may not have any legal qualifications or training are the least regulated.'
>
> 'The problem is exacerbated by the fact that the title 'lawyer' is not legally protected. Anyone can call themselves a lawyer or offer legal services as a lawyer, irrespective of whether they have any legal training or qualifications. This is confusing for the public and in some cases misleading.'
>
> 'We believe, therefore, that professional standards should be set by the profession; by the people who understand

---

123 28 January 2016
124 Times 28 January 2016
125 15 February 2016

what 'good' looks like and want to differentiate themselves (on the basis of a higher standard) from other non-professional but regulated, legal services.'

'In this context, consideration needs to be given to which activities are reserved to the legal profession, because higher standards of professional behaviour and conduct apply there ... these include but are not limited to, litigation and advocacy, and the ability to give advice which is legally privileged because the role of solicitors as officers of the court means that they have a professional duty to the court.'

'Effectively public protection can only be assured if freedom from government intervention is an essential cornerstone of our justice system and underpins the rule of law.'

They are all coming to the same conclusion that I foresaw when I started this book. In other words 'I told you so.'

But the truth of the matter is, that we will continue. There are still young people who want to go into the profession with the aim of helping others. There are still some who feel that advocacy is something that is in their nature and is what they want to do by way of a profession or trade

The trouble is that it is becoming more like a trade than a profession and the constant pressure on the financial aspects of being a common attorney does mean that the concentration on the client's affairs is not the same as it was in my 'old days'.

The number of aspiring young men or women who would like to set up their own practice must be virtually nil. Not only is there the three-year restriction, but also the thought of trying to run a solicitor's practice, keep up with the law, help your clients, and also comply with the quite amazing amount of administration and checks, that you have to carry out, is an impediment to anyone wanting to start their own practice. The cost of doing so, is also high.

Not only is there the cost of the practicing certificate but also the great spectre of indemnity insurance. In addition, if you want to have a reasonable library then you either have to pay quite a lot of money, to be able to subscribe to a major book on the web or alternatively buy one at an even higher price. Of course, there are benefits for Joe Public because there are all these checks and there is the guarantee that a solicitor has been in practice for a few years, before he starts to 'operate' on the client.

In a thought provoking article,[126] Joanna Goodman described the views and methods of some who are keeping the flame burning, she wrote:

> 'Although the High Street has experienced its share of losses, these need to be considered, alongside the various failures and distressed mergers, involving mid market and larger firms. Furthermore, after huge initial investment and a relatively short honeymoon period, not all the big commercial enterprises are thriving. This year saw Stobart Barristers close its doors and Co-operative Legal Services, which was the first ABS to be approved by the SRA, reported losses of £1.5m for the first half of this year.'
> 'I take a different perspective on the battle for the high street, to identify how technology, rather than driving the extinction of High Street practices, has become one of the main weapons in their armoury. Technology has enabled them to strengthen their market presence and client relationships; enhance, deliver and promote their services: and differentiate themselves from faceless commercial enterprises entering the legal services market.'

She refers to Brian Inkster of Inksters in Glasgow

> 'who has created a powerful online presence for himself and his firm, through Twitter and his blog, The Time Blawg. Inksters' strategic use of technology, enables a firm which employs just 16 people to handle specialist crofting work and compete for high street business, throughout Scot-

---

126 LSG 22 September 2014

land. 'Online legal services are looking to capture everyone, while high street firms concentrate on local markets and niche work. It's about focusing on geography and capturing the people who are looking for you,'

She says:

'The differentiator for local law firms in terms of competitive advantage, is that they get closer to their clients than any commercial enterprise can, and that they can use technology to leverage and enhance this.
'Social media enables us to get closer to our clients than ever before,' she observes, 'It means that we can give them the service that they really want.'
And quoting another firm:
'communication is the glue that binds high street firms to their communities – their clients and their peers. And taking advantage of online communication is central to the entrepreneurial legal services models that are keeping the High Street alive.'

And Roger Smith, who I have already quoted, when reviewing the report of a survey by Ipsos Mori amongst solicitors, noted[127] that:

'The report is ... strong ... on the need for practices to innovate and improve their managements. Indeed, the latter is one of the few glimmers of light – 57% of those surveyed are not hopeful about the future of the profession and 69% would not recommend joining it. But, at least the Titanic is going down with the deck chairs better arraigned: 74% think that their legal practices are better than five years ago. And only a party-pooping sceptic would

---

127 LSG 298 September 2015

note that 83% of the survey sample consisted of partners, managing partners and heads of chambers.'

And another spark? 'A new consolidator has vowed to acquire 60 high street law firms, within five years' so announced the Law Society website.[128] The creator of the concept explained in management speak:

> 'We are just about to start the technology and change management process pilot and the nature of the input and resources ...'

To which a reader responded:

> 'Net result? Rubbish service but delicious economies of scale. We shall see but don't say I didn't warn you.'

I don't know who is correct so I shall place my bet 'each way'.

So the answer is six of one and half a dozen of the other. Some things are better, some things are worse, but the profession will still struggle on, and I hope, forever.

---

128 27 May 2015

CHAPTER 11

A NIGHTMARE SCENARIO

What if I (and Susskind) am wrong? What could be left?

There could be a world where most house transactions are a carried out by Licensed Conveyancers – or banks or haulage companies.

There could be a world where will writers drafted most wills, and probate is obtained by accountants and banks who also administer most estates. It may be even worse. One of the 'big four' firms of accountants is forging ahead with the expansion of its legal services plan. Their EY Global leader says they are:

> 'not directly competing with the business model of the traditional law firms'[129]

He would, wouldn't he?

There will still be scope for a few highly organised solicitors to deal with licensing, but there will be little for the high street guy to bother to get involved in, in such a technical world.

There may be just a few dedicated lawyers, who want to help poor distressed men and women, who want to end their marriages, in the least painful way and some who are dedicated to looking after the interests of children. But as they rarely can get paid by legal aid or by the client, they will be impoverished solicitors, wondering if they can remain solvent. They will have a difficult time trying to cope with the many litigants in person.

There will be solicitors who stand up in the criminal courts to represent those whose liberty is at stake. Cheaper, less quali-

---

129 LSG 1 June 2015

fied Mackenzie friends will be competing with them, having obtained the right to offer direct access by the public. A few barristers, probably those with private incomes, or supportive families, will be available, hoping that, as ever, they will be preferred over solicitors, when there are judicial vacancies available.

There will be still be many well paid members of firms who can help sort out the arguments of those who can afford to pay them. For small disputes, the litigant in person will decide that he cannot get legal aid and cannot afford a lawyer, He will be represented by Mackenzie friends or rely on such assistance as might be offered by the Court Service. They may be able to find help on the net but the only common attorneys who can offer help, are those who do a little pro bono work in a big commercial firm or a chap working from his bedroom at home.

There will be the so called fat cats, who deal with all commercial matters, which will be one of the few fields where the solicitor with direct contact with his client, will reign supreme but it is unlikely to filter down to the high street solicitor.

So imagine the poor lawyer. Yes a poor lawyer. He will sit before his client, in his cold office, wearing worn out clothes. He is probably wondering, as he tries to concentrate on his client's problem, about his own. Should he close up? It will not be the end of his woes[130]. It will be the common attorney who will be tearful not the client. The client will comfort the poor tattered lawyer, but he will tell him that he still believes that a man who has himself as a lawyer, will have a fool for a client,

I found this on the Internet from Sam Blackman:-

A young clerk was fed up with the law.

So he packed up and went for the door.

---

[130] If he had been negligent in the last six years he will remain liable in damages but his insurance might have expired. The Law Society is contemplating a hardship fund to help pay so called run – off insurance costs if the solicitor passes a 'hardship test'. (Law Society Press Release 9 July 2015)

Said his colleagues to him, 'This decision is dim!'
He replied: 'You just wait what's in store'!"

After that nightmare I hope to wake up to see a less dramatic picture.

ACKNOWLEMENTS

I am grateful to a number of my colleagues who have much more up to date knowledge and experience than me, who have been willing to look at some parts of this work. They include:

Murray Schifeldrin, Norman Taylor, Carl Gallagher, Andrew Hougie, Russell Graham and Michael Lewin

I thank them all but would stress that if there are any errors in subjects which are their particular specialties then those errors are my alone.

Rate this book on our website!

www.novum-publishing.co.uk

The author

Jerry Pearlman resides in Leeds and is married with two children, now aged 51 and 53. Now in his 80s, Jerry has decided to take a look back on his long and successful career through the writing of his second book, The Death of the Common Attorney. A keen walker, Jerry is an honorary Vice President of the Ramblers, as well as a Parish Councillor and the Chairman of the Yorkshire and Humber Regional Access Forum. Professionally, he has been the President of his local Law Society, and a member of the Solicitors Complaints Bureau. He was awarded the M.B.E. for his services to the Ramblers Association.

novum PUBLISHER FOR NEW AUTHORS

The publisher

> *He who stops being better stops being good.*

This is the motto of novum publishing, and our focus is on finding new manuscripts, publishing them and offering long-term support to the authors.
Our publishing house was founded in 1997, and since then it has become THE expert for new authors and has won numerous awards.

Our editorial team will peruse each manuscript within a few weeks free of charge and without obligation.

You will find more information about
novum publishing and our books on the internet:

w w w . n o v u m - p u b l i s h i n g . c o . u k